THE BREATHINGBOOK
for singers

Bonnie Draina

The Breathing Book for Singers
Bonnie Draina

MPM 00-001
$19.95
© 2019 Mountain Peak Music

2700 Woodlands Village Blvd. #300-124
Flagstaff, Arizona 86001
www.mountainpeakmusic.com

ISBN 978-1-935510-94-9

Images used by permission:

© David Gorman from *The Body Moveable* (www.bodymoveable.com): pages 1 and 19 (the skull, cervical spine, and trachea), 3 (facial muscles), 7 (the ribs and diaphragm), 20 (neck muscles), 22 (the spine), 34 (the ribs, costal cartilage, and sternum), 36 (levator costarum and intercostal muscles), 37 (serratus anterior muscles), 44 (vocal tract from behind), 47 (right arm front and back view), 49 (the diaphragm, ribs and spine from below), 58 (strained and collapsed postures)

© Holly Fischer / Andover Educators: page 4 (views of the lungs), 13 (outline), 14 (outline with skeleton), 20 (posterior view of A-O and atlas-axis joints), 23 (sitting in balance), 25 (the pelvis in context and lateral male pelvis), 26 (the diaphragm and pelvic floor), 27 (anterior male pelvis and anterior female pelvis), 29 (lateral and medial views of the left foot and posterior heel - right foot), 30 (lateral right knee), 31 (anterior view of the right leg), 33 (the ribs and spine), 39 (abdominal muscles), 48 (right arm - supination and pronation), 53 (upper leg/diaphragm relationship and pelvic floor), 57 (leaning forward in balance upright)

© Benjamin Conable: page 8 (the ribs and diaphragm - side view), 39 (abdominal space cross section), 43 (the tongue, mouth and throat), 45 (cross section of the neck)

© Bourgery and Jacob - from *Anatomie de l'homme,* Paris: Guérin Ed., 1862 (https://commons.m.wikimedia.org/wiki/File:Bourgery_%26_Jacob.jpg): page 5 (the heart and lungs)

© Albinus - from *Tabulae sceleti et musculorum corporis humani*, London: Typis H. Woodfall, impensis Johannis et Pauli Knapton, 1749 (https://www.nlm.nih.gov/exhibition/historicalanatomies/albinus_home.html): page 46 (poised arms)

© Amy Likar: page 50 (exploration on a ball), 51 (explorations one and two with a pillow)

© Blandine Calais-Germain - from *The Anatomy of Breathing*: 40 (abdominal space cut-away)

Table of Contents

Foreword

The "singer breath," or breathing in general, has been the subject of almost mythical proportions over approximately two centuries of vocal pedagogy. The occasional listener often asks "How do they do that?" The student most assuredly asks "How should I be doing that?"

It is my pleasure to introduce this very "non-mythical," extremely concise and informative book about breath, breathing, and other very useful anatomical facts necessary for singers—and certainly appropriate for all human beings.

> *"The foundation of all vocal study lies in the control of the breath."*
> Giovanni Battista Lamperti

How often have we heard from well-meaning coaches, teachers and even conductors to "sing from the diaphragm" or to "support your tone more"? These two comments are the tips of very complex icebergs, if you will, that this guide will help you navigate.

The teaching of singing is not mystical. It is the distilled understanding of our natural physical and emotional abilities to express ourselves in a language called music. We as singers, physically—athletically in fact—make human thoughts audible through this musical language. How, you may ask? Well, reading this book is a good start to finding your answer.

Over the years I have enjoyed a very rewarding teaching schedule in addition to my performance calendar. I have always enjoyed passing along knowledge from the very particular sources of my own vocal education, starting with an acute knowledge of yoga, pilates, Alexander Technique and other various physical disciplines. These disciplines were fundamental to the beginning of my singing career and were self-understood for a life on the stage. For this, I am eternally grateful.

Therefore, it has always been surprising to me, while addressing a very enthusiastic group of young singers in the latest master class I am giving, to ask a "trick" question: "How many keys does a piano keyboard have?" Immediately, and without fail, comes a unanimous answer: 88. (Some well-studied young scholar always offers the addendum of the famous Bösendorfer piano, with its four extra keys.)

But then I ask: "How many ribs do you have?" There is always an awkward silence. Then, the guessing starts: "9?", "16?", "Ah, different in men and women." (This last one is my favorite answer, ha ha! The real answer is on page 33.)

The story told above is typically heard today in singer conversations around the world. I find this astounding, and that is part of my great enthusiasm for this book, which joins the growing number of new works of performance literature aimed at the practical, realizable study of what singers need to know about their body.

I was very fortunate to have been introduced to yoga during my university studies. Being a very athletic young man, this new world of mind and body was revelatory to me and became elemental to my maturation as a singing artist as I learned to balance both professional and personal demands on my body as an instrument.

It's never too late to embrace the admonition of Meribeth Dayme:

> *"The voice and body are full of logic and common sense. Learning to think for yourself, rather than panic about the unknown, is the first step in developing and keeping a healthy voice."*

The facts of our anatomical structure are not "mystical," and in fact understanding—and visualizing—your body's structure and function will directly inform the inspirational in your performing.

Know your body—sing your heart—resonate your soul: WHAT A LIFE!

Fortune favors the prepared mind.

Good luck!

Thomas Hampson

Acknowledgements

The Breathing Book for Singers is the latest in a series that began with Barbara Conable's groundbreaking primer, *The Structures and Movement of Breathing,* and David Vining's *The Breathing Book for Tuba*. I am honored that two such pioneers entrusted this volume to me and am deeply grateful for their guidance and patience along the way. My sincere thanks go to other Body Mapping authors, especially Amy Likar and Melissa Malde, for helping me find just the right words. I truly appreciate Holly Fischer, Benjamin Conable and David Gorman, whose illustrations are so crucial to the impact of this book. The experiential format I chose was inspired by Blandine Calais-Germaine's uniquely interactive anatomy books, and I am delighted that she granted the use of one of her own illustrations.

The resources provided by several professional organizations were instrumental in forming the knowledge base for this book: many thanks to Andover Educators, The National Association of Teachers of Singing, Performing Arts Medicine Association and The Voice Foundation.

For the energy, enthusiasm and expertise freely shared by so many, making possible this book and my life in music, I offer thanks to: Jaime Stover Schmitt and Barbara Conable, who started me along this path by teaching me to move with awareness and inspiring me to teach others; my wonderful colleagues in our collaborative community of Andover Educators, especially Quinn Patrick, Kurt-Alexander Zeller, MaryJean Allen, Kay Hooper, Doug Johnson and Melanie Sever; Lucille Reilly for enthusiastic guidance to this novice author; Peggy Baroody, Kate Emerich and Anat Keidar for sharing their profound knowledge of the voice; Liz Stewart, Lissa Joy, Al Wadleigh and Wendy Bramlett for a deeper appreciation of my own moving body; Marvin Keenze and Jim Brody for carefully guiding my pedagogical development; Stephen Bruns for prompting me to write authoritatively; Laura Greenwald, Lorna MacDonald, Margaret Cusack and Julie Simson for supportive, joyous singing lessons; Martin Néron, Michael Tilley, Sarah Parkinson, Mutsumi Moteki, and so many wonderful musical partners; Meribeth Dayme, Stephen Smith, Jeanette LoVetri and a long list of inspiring vocal pedagogues; my creative collaborators in nurturing the whole musician, especially Jeremy Dittus, Matthew Tomatz, John Crever and Joanne Racciatti-Parker; Luisa Rodriguez, Jackie Grigg, Garrett Smith, Nicole London, Elizabeth Whitney, Janet Braccio, Kathy Stith, Laura Chyn and hundreds more students whose questions and talents have kept me engaged and honest; Mom, Dad and Nancy for a home full of music, crafts and love; Matt Heck, whose faith in me and relentless interest in singing and somatics are continually inspiring; and to Rio, for living with joyful abandon and giving Mama time to write.

Introduction

The purpose of *The Breathing Book for Singers* is to encourage more expressive and enjoyable singing through a deep understanding of the vocal instrument: the body in motion. Singers with a fluid physical awareness are liberated singers. Freed from nagging thoughts about "correct" posture or breathing, they can focus on the expressive and musical elements of singing. Artistic inspiration leads them to take just the right breath for each phrase. That breath honors the music while also honoring the body's need for oxygen.

Singing is movement. For every vocal sound we can imagine, there is a unique combination of physical movements to create that sound. Variations in musical elements such as timbre, articulation and dynamics result from variations in movement.

How we move is determined to a great degree by our body maps. These maps are self-representations in our mind of our structure (what we are like), function (what we do) and size (how big we are). We map our whole bodies and we map our parts. When these maps are integrated and accurate, movement is comfortable and coordinated.

We create our body maps in infancy through exploration and observation. Ideally, we continue to revise these maps as our bodies change throughout our lives. However, just as a road map may be accurate, slightly outdated or just plain wrong, body maps also vary in accuracy. When our body maps are a little bit off, movement is awkward or uncomfortable. When our body maps are utterly wrong, we are prone to pain and injury.

Instructions we hear as singers often include words like "support," "appoggio," and "sub-glottal pressure." Without a clear understanding of what those directions mean within our bodies, we often respond with overwork. Whether the resulting physical tension is felt in the throat, abdomen, legs or elsewhere, it negatively affects breathing and vocal sound. The good news is that we can access, assess and adjust our body maps to improve our movement and the musical results.

Your body maps may currently be operating at an unconscious level so that you are unaware of the contents or their effects on your movement and singing. Through inquiry and examination, you can bring your maps into consciousness and explore their accuracy. With awareness and observation, you can make corrections where necessary, leading to better movement. Soon you may find that you can give more attention to artistic thoughts in performance because your body responds to those ideas with spontaneous, integrated movement.

To gain the most from this book, I encourage you to experience it fully. Simply reading and learning the information intellectually will not change your maps or improve your movement. Body Mapping requires a rich sensory experience to activate neurological changes, so this book is designed to help you fully absorb the truth about various aspects of breathing. The first section of each chapter presents information about breathing through illustrations and text. The

"Sense" and "Sing" segments that follow contain activities to help you begin exploring and revising your body maps immediately. Simple musical exercises are presented in medium keys; you should feel free to transpose and modify them to better match your own vocal style and range. Once you have tried the suggested exercises, you may wish to augment them with explorations of your own devising.

When you first created your body maps as a baby, you experimented with movement and experienced your body through many senses. Those same processes will serve you well here. Experiment and play! As your maps improve, so will your movement, whether you are singing or dancing, knitting, running or rock climbing. Enjoy!

I. Personal Cartography - Body Mapping Basics

Body Mapping is a process that may only take a few moments for one person, while for another it might take weeks to make permanent changes in a map. One aspect of mapping is true for everyone, though: it requires active attention to the body in motion. It is not enough to learn intellectually about a part of your body that is giving you trouble. In order for your maps to change, your brain must clearly perceive movement in and around the part in question, and it must make changes based on that perception.

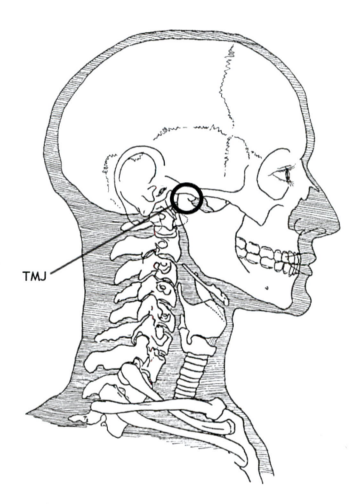

1.1 the skull, cervical spine and trachea

The first step in Body Mapping is to recognize movement difficulty. For example, you may notice that your jaw muscles are tense when you inhale or that you are not able to open your mouth easily for an "ah" vowel. Once you have identified a problem, it is time to put on your detective hat and start asking some questions. You might look at anatomical illustrations similar to figure 1.1 and wonder, "Does that picture match my own map? Does anything in this drawing look odd to me?" For example, does the location of the temporo-mandibular joint (TMJ) in the illustration match your own map of your TMJs? Many singers have flawed maps of these joints; as a result they may experience muscular tension or pain, noisy breathing, impaired diction or resonance, or even injury.

A single round of questioning, examining and exploring may be all it takes to fix the problem you initially identified. However, you might need to reinforce the new map many times for changes to occur. Think of it as taking the time to completely erase an old map and clearly draw a new one. If after a week of Body Mapping you still feel some tension or awkwardness in the area in question, another round of mapping in the same area or a neighboring one may be in order. Be persistent, be curious, and enjoy the resulting improvements in your movement and sound!

All sections of this book are designed to inspire repeated "rounds" of Body Mapping—feeling your movement, correcting your map as needed, sensing the improvement you have made and clearly identifying how you made the improvement so that it becomes permanent—with plenty of illustrations and exercises to get you started in the process.

Before You Begin

It is important that your body maps accurately reflect your own unique body. When looking at anatomical drawings and models, keep in mind that your structure may vary somewhat from those depicted. For example, your own mandible may be longer or broader than the one in the picture, or the disc in one or both of your TMJs may be displaced or damaged in some way. These differences may be due to genetic influence, injury, or habits such as clenching the teeth. This book will guide you in using your senses to map your own structure accurately.

Body Mapping is intended to help you perceive and map your own body accurately so that you can move as easily and efficiently as possible. If Body Mapping does not seem to be helping, or if you experience frequent pain or numbness, please seek help from a doctor or other qualified professional.

Let's get familiar with the process of Body Mapping by exploring the jaw.

Sense

1. Take a moment to access your own map of your TMJs—where do you imagine your jaw attaches to your skull? Put your fingertips where you think the joints are, then look at figure 1.1 and see what you notice. The two TMJs are much closer to the ears than many people suppose.

2. With figure 1.1 as a guide, use your fingertips to find the actual location of the joints. Notice how close your TMJs are to your cheekbones and how far they are from your lips. Feel the movement under your fingertips as you gently open and close your jaw, move your jaw forward, back and side to side.

3. Palpate along your jawline until your fingers meet in the front. Notice that you have one jaw, but you have two joints where the jaw articulates with the skull. How do the shape and size of your jaw compare with the illustration? Each person is unique.

4. Open and close your jaw gently, paying attention to the internal feeling of the movement. What muscles are active when you open your mouth wide? Do those muscles need to work when you open your mouth only slightly, or can you let gravity do the work for you? Do you feel muscles working when you close your mouth? The primary jaw-closing muscles, the masseters, are very strong. They are active in chewing, closing and clenching the jaw. Use

figure 1.2 as a guide to explore your masseter muscles.

5. Say "ah" and try to sense exactly how far you have opened your mouth. Check in the mirror or with your fingertips to see how accurately you felt your movement. Repeat this exercise with other vowels, singing and speaking. You will learn more about movement perception in Chapter Four, *The Sixth Sense*.

Sing

Sing a familiar warm-up routine with special attention to your jaw. Use these guidelines to focus your exploration. As you come up with other ideas, go ahead and experiment!

1. For the first minute or two, monitor the movement of your TMJs with your fingertips.

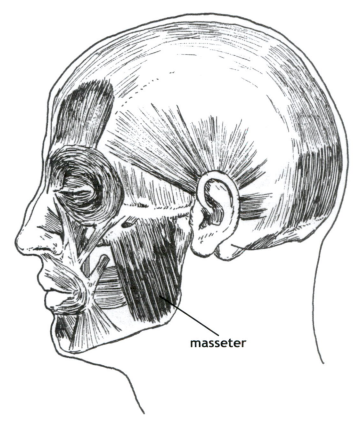

1.2 facial muscles

2. Notice if you feel any tension in your tongue, jaw or neck muscles during inhalation. Allow that tension to release. Does your breathing change? Your singing?

3. Sense how far you are opening your mouth as you sing. Use a mirror or your fingertips to check, as well as your internal movement sense.

If all of this attention to movement has made you more attentive to your jaw's joints, muscles and movement, enjoy this awareness—it will help refine your body maps.

Popping or clicking in one or both TMJs can indicate a problem with the joints and should be discussed with your teacher or dentist. For resources to help with more detailed mapping of your jaw, see the Appendix.

II. Where the Air Goes - Your Lungs

Where exactly the lungs are and what they do is a bit of a mystery to many singers. The lungs take up most of the thoracic cavity, from slightly above the collarbones down to the bottom of the sternum. Sharing the inner rib space only with the heart and a few major vessels, the lungs take up all that space, from side to side and front to back.

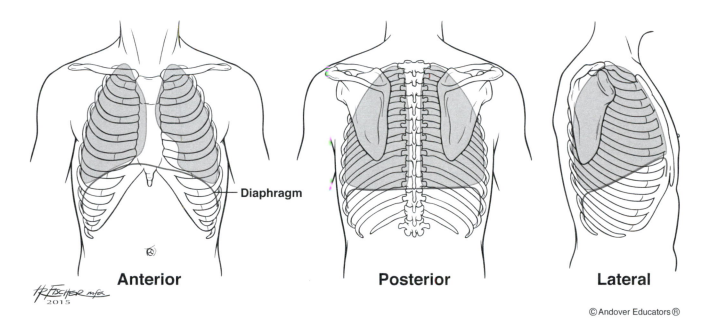

2.1 views of the lungs

The lungs are not in the belly, as many singers imagine. Breathing does involve abdominal movement, but air never goes into your abdomen, no matter how "low" you breathe. Air travels through the pharyngeal space, past the vocal folds, and through the trachea on its way to the lungs. Notice in figure 2.2 that the trachea divides into progressively smaller channels, taking air to all parts of the lungs. When you inhale, air diffuses throughout the lungs; it does not fill the bottom of the lungs first, as though it were water, another common misconception. How you choose to breathe will affect the distribution of the air to some degree, but air always enters the lungs from this central place behind the sternum.

The lungs themselves are comprised of intricately folded layers of super-fine tissue that facilitate the exchange of gases to keep us alive and healthy. They are not hollow like balloons. Lung tissue is very elastic and springy, but lungs cannot move themselves! Instead, they go along with the flow of movement all around them. If you have mistakenly mapped the lungs as pressing out against the ribs and diaphragm, be sure to revise your maps to include lungs that *are moved by* the surrounding structures. We will explore those moving structures in the pages ahead.

We inhale fresh air to bring oxygen into the body, and our exhalation carries carbon dioxide out. To achieve peak performance, singers must breathe in a way that supports respiration as well as phonation. An olympic athlete would never choose a breathing method that prevents optimal oxygenation of the body and brain, but singers frequently do just that. When we habitually take in more air than we can use in a phrase, then inhale fresh air on top of stale air, oxygen levels decline and carbon dioxide levels rise in the body. This process leads to imbalances in blood chemistry and poor performance. You can breathe to support life optimally and sing beautifully on the exhaust!

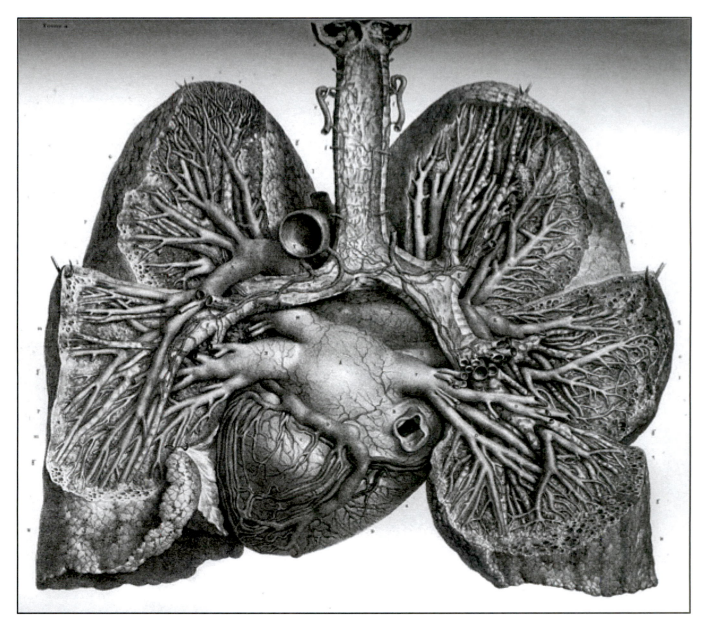

2.2 the heart and lungs

Sense

1. Refer to figure 2.1 as you explore the size of your lungs. Rest your fingertips on your collarbones to point at the tops of your lungs. Walk your fingertips down the front of your sternum to sense how "tall" your lungs are.

2. Notice that in figure 2.1 the bottom of the lungs is lower in back than in front. Use your hands to feel how deep and wide the thoracic space is within your ribs. That space is taken up completely by your lungs, heart and vessels such as the aorta.

3. Notice the location and size of your trachea just below your larynx. (See figure 1.1 for a side view of the trachea.) Place your fingertips in the soft notch just above your sternum, then feel the trachea extending upward from there. Gently walk your fingertips up along your trachea a few inches until you reach your larynx.

4. Spend a few minutes exploring that area of your neck. Notice the rings of cartilage that form your trachea. This strong, flexible tube is always open and always filled with air. As you breathe, acknowledge the air passing just under your fingertips. Food and drink pass through your esophagus *behind* your trachea.

5. Tap the center of your sternum with your fingertips. Just behind your sternum your trachea branches out into the bronchial tubes and then into ever smaller vessels. Those vessels lead to about 300 million alveoli where the exchange of oxygen and carbon dioxide occurs. Figure 2.2 clearly shows the intimate connection of the respiratory and circulatory systems. The alveoli are rich in elastic connective tissue that allows your lungs to shift shape and size with the movement of your breath and then spring back, much like a sponge.

6. Inhale, then simply relax and allow an "elastic" exhalation that feels like a sigh. Experiment with the speed and size of your inhalation. Notice how the quality of the resulting exhalation changes.

Sing

1. As you sing a familiar song, rest your fingertips on your trachea. Gently feel the rings of cartilage in the very front of your neck, just below your larynx. Remind yourself that the trachea is always open and always full of air.

2. Sing a single note until you are comfortably nearing the end of your breath, then breathe and repeat. Nourish your brain and your sound.

III. The Truth About the Diaphragm

The diaphragm is the primary muscle of inhalation. It is on the job 24/7, whether we are asleep or awake. Unfortunately, many singers are unable to breathe easily because their map of the diaphragm is faulty. Consider this experience: A teacher or conductor exhorts us to "sing from the diaphragm" while pointing to an area somewhere near the belly button, then directs us to do some form of panting or pulsing of the abdomen. As a result of this and other well-intended instructions, many singers begin to think of the diaphragm as a belt-like muscle that contracts to push air out of the body. This notion could not be further from the truth!

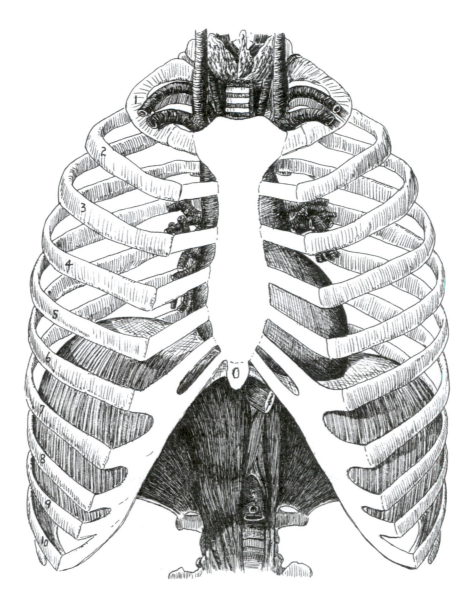

3.1 the ribs and diaphragm

As you can see in figure 3.1, the diaphragm is a thin, dome-shaped layer of strong muscle and connective tissue. It curves up inside the ribs, slightly higher on the right side than the left. The diaphragm separates the thoracic and abdominal cavities, with the lungs and heart sitting atop it and the liver and other organs nestled up underneath it. The bottom edge of the diaphragm is attached to the inner surface of the lower ribs all the way around, and it is anchored to the front of the lumbar spine by muscle fibers and tendons. At the top and center of the diaphragm, the muscle fibers radiate down and out from the central tendon, seen as a white area in figure 3.2. Dark lines show the orientation of the fibers.

When your brain signals a need for oxygen, or when you form an intention to sing or speak, these muscle fibers contract and the dome-shaped diaphragm becomes more shallow as its circumference increases. As the diaphragm moves, it pulls down on the heart and lungs. The action of the diaphragm also helps the lower ribs to swing up and away from the spine. These movements increase the volume of the thoracic cavity, causing air to flow into the lungs. How much air enters the lungs depends upon how far the diaphragm and ribs move to enlarge the lungs. The important message here is that contraction of the diaphragm causes *inhalation*.

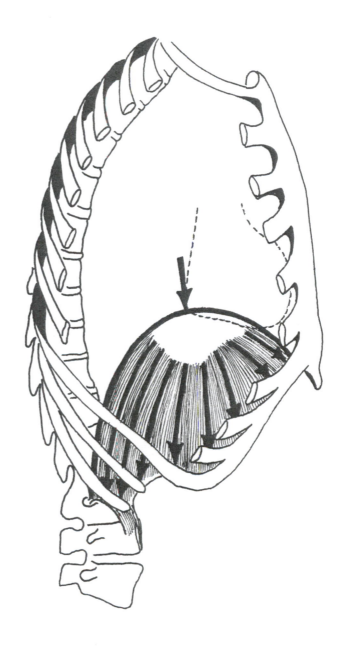

3.2 the ribs and diaphragm (side view)

The diaphragm moves in opposition to and in cooperation with other muscle groups. As you inhale, the diaphragm's movement coordinates with muscles moving the ribs, spine and sternum to widen and deepen the thoracic cavity and draw in air. While the diaphragm is pulling down on the lungs and heart, it is also pushing down on the organs below, creating outward pressure on the muscles of the abdomen and pelvis. Each of these muscle groups is featured in another chapter. Get to know them all and how they support your singing through beautiful, buoyant breathing!

Sense

1. Look at the illustrations and see what you notice. Do your internal maps include a diaphragm that is large and domed, as in the pictures? Or do you think of your diaphragm more like a belt or cummerbund? Do you allow easy movement of your diaphragm during inhalation, or have you been trying to use your diaphragm to exhale?

2. Use your fingertips to trace the lower edge of your diaphragm. Starting in front at the bottom of your sternum, walk your fingers along the lower edge of your ribs all the way around to your spine. Look at the drawings as you explore and notice that your diaphragm is anchored on the inside of your lower ribs, just millimeters from your fingertips.

3. Because the diaphragm does not contain proprioceptive nerve endings, we cannot control or feel its movement directly. However, we can feel it indirectly as it affects other areas of the body. Hold your nose, close your mouth and gently try to inhale. Although no air is entering your body, you will feel movement throughout your torso as your diaphragm and other breathing muscles contract. Do you feel movement in your abdomen or pelvic floor? That movement is a result of your diaphragm pressing down on your abdominal organs. Is there movement in your back? Lower ribs? Some of that movement will be due to the diaphragm's effect on the lower ribs, and some will be caused by back and rib muscles working to help you breathe. If you feel tension in your neck, shoulders or legs during this exercise, allow those muscles to relax as you repeat the exercise gently.

4. Watch a video of the diaphragm and ribs in motion (see Appendix). Notice the coordinated movement of the ribs and diaphragm. Spend some time breathing along with the video - inhale as the diaphragm contracts to move down and out, then exhale as it releases and domes back up. Use your hands to feel the movement of your ribs and abdomen as you breathe. Notice the quality of your movement—is breathing easy? Can you release tension in your abdomen, neck or arms that will allow more ease and freedom in your breathing?

Sing

Sing these scales in an easy range. Remind yourself that your diaphragm is contracting as you inhale and releasing as you sing. Place your hands on your abdomen or watch yourself in a mirror to feel and see movements in your torso to reinforce that idea.

Sing in a key that accommodates your vocal range.

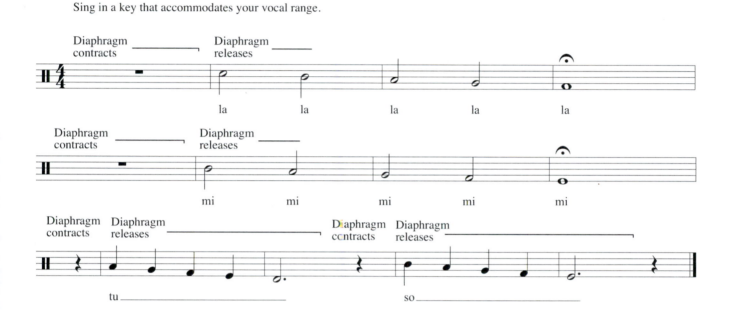

IV. The Sixth Sense - Movement and Kinesthesia

During childhood we were taught that there are five major senses: sight, sound, taste, smell and touch. Unfortunately, most of us did not learn about the movement sense, kinesthesia, so we may just ignore it. To move, breathe and sing well, it is essential that we start paying attention!

The kinesthetic sense sends the brain information about the body's movement. The sense receptors are in the connective tissues of our muscles and concentrated around our joints. Just as our ears provide information about whether we are singing flat, sharp or in tune, soft or loud, dark or bright, our kinesthetic sense receptors tell us if our muscles are contracting or relaxed, moving a lot or a little, easily or with effort. We are able to respond to auditory information to change our sound. We can also respond to kinesthetic information to bring ourselves to optimal movement.

The kinesthetic sense is interoceptive. In other words, it gives the brain information about our own body. It tells us about the quality and degree of our movements and the position and size of our body. The other main senses, which are exteroceptive, primarily provide information about the world around us. In order to know what we are doing while we sing, we must pay attention to the kinesthetic sense. You may think you are opening your mouth fully to sing that "ah" vowel, but if you are ignoring the movement sense you won't know for sure unless you look in the mirror!

During singing, the kinesthetic sense allows us to monitor important activities such as lip and tongue movement, the quality of gestures and facial expressions, and the amount and speed of our breath. If we ignore this information, whether intentionally or not, singing becomes haphazard and unpredictable. Dancers and athletes cannot expect excellent performance without attending to their movement sense, and neither can musicians.

The kinesthetic sense is also an important tool for developing and modifying our body maps. When we allow our brain to notice and respond to kinesthetic sensory input, we are able to correct and refine our body maps effectively. Kinesthesia helps us move, breathe and sing well. As vocal pedagogue and somatic pioneer Jeanette LoVetri says, "You have to move it to feel it, and feel it to move it!"

Sense

1. To explore the kinesthetic sense, raise one hand above your head. Wiggle your fingers without looking at your hand. Your kinesthetic sense receptors will give you information about how quickly, how easily and how far you are moving your fingers. The tactile, or touch, sense will tell you if your fingers touch and how the air feels against your skin. Are you able to sense the speed at which your fingers are moving? How hard are your muscles working to

move your fingers? Does your arm feel tense or loose? If your pinky finger suddenly grew longer, your kinesthetic sense would tell you.

2. Notice if you are able to easily distinguish kinesthetic (movement) information from tactile (touch). You may have been ignoring kinesthetic input for many years, but attending to it now will help your brain recognize it more readily.

3. Rub your thumbs and fingertips together. Are you able to feel activity in your muscles and joints while also noticing the texture and shape of your fingertips?

4. Stand up and windmill both arms. Can you feel movement in the joints of your spine, legs or any other parts of your body? Do you notice tactile sensations where your clothes are touching your skin?

5. Notice if your balance is shifting over your feet as you move your arms. Tactile sense receptors on the surface of your feet are sending your brain information about weight and pressure, while kinesthetic receptors in the connective tissue of your feet and legs are telling you about muscle and joint activity.

Sing

As you sing these exercises, use your kinesthetic sense to gather information about your body. Notice whether the muscles in the area indicated feel tight or free. If you sense tension, respond by bringing yourself into balance and freeing the muscles of extra work. Does your sound change as a result?

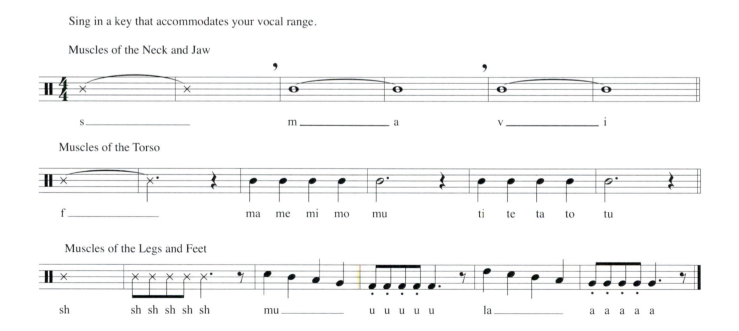

Sing in a key that accommodates your vocal range.

Muscles of the Neck and Jaw

Muscles of the Torso

Muscles of the Legs and Feet

V. Finding Balance - Your Skeleton

To breathe and sing well, it is important to have an adequate and accurate map of our whole skeleton. The skeleton provides a framework and sturdy support for all of the movements of singing. When our bones are aligned and balanced, our muscles are free to move.

Optimal alignment is crucial to good singing, so singers spend a lot of time thinking about posture. However, judgments about posture tend to be visual: Are your shoulders back? Are your feet in the right position? Trying to meet those external expectations often leads to physical tension, which is just another way of saying "extra work for your muscles." Finding alignment or balance, on the other hand, requires that you notice how your body feels: Is your neck tense or free? Are you balanced over your feet?

Once the body is aligned, with all parts in agreement, movement is easier and more efficient. Unlike posture, we don't *hold* alignment or balance. It is a state we continually move through and return to as we sing or carry out any activity. In fact, when we are aligned and our muscles are free, our bodies are in a constant state of micro-movement. Automatic reflexes continually bring us back to balance, even when we appear to be standing still. When our body maps are accurate and we are kinesthetically aware, balance becomes easy to find and we no longer need to think about "posture."

Sense

1. Without looking at the next page, draw a skeleton in the outline in figure 5.1. Don't worry about how perfect or artistic your drawing might be. Rely on your innate understanding of your own skeleton as you draw. How big are your bones? What are your knees like? Are your ribs attached to anything? And so on.

2. Once you have finished drawing, open the book and compare the skeleton you drew with the one in figure 5.2. What is the same? What is different? Did you draw a

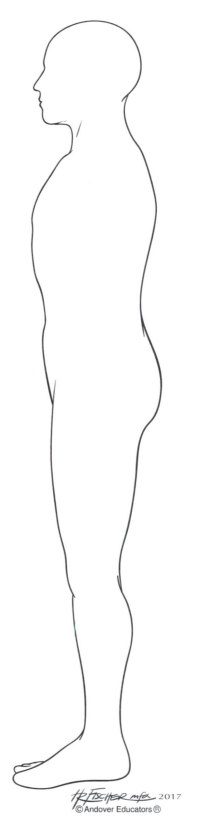

5.1 outline

13

straight, skinny spine right along the back of the body? How do the skull, spine and jaw you drew relate to one another? Did you draw an upper arm bone that has a joint with the shoulder blade? Are the ribs you drew parallel with the ground or angled? What are the ribs attached to in the back? In the front? Did you draw a thigh bone that articulates with the pelvis? Did you draw a pelvis at all? How did you draw the knee? Are the feet you drew flat blocks or arched and flexible? What else do you notice?

3. Use a different color pencil to circle or re-draw the areas that need improvement.

Comparing your drawing with figure 5.2 provides you with important information about your body maps and movement habits. For example, if you drew a skinny spine right at the back of the torso, you very likely stand with your weight thrown back. This posture tightens muscles throughout your body, including muscles involved in breathing. Correcting that skeletal map and others will make it easier to find balance and improve your breathing.

Our skeletons provide a structure of support and weight distribution. When our bones are optimally aligned, they are able to deliver our weight to the ground with little or no muscular help. Figure 5.2 shows a beautifully balanced skeleton. From the base up, we see the whole body balanced over the arches of the feet, the thigh bones balanced over the lower legs, the torso balanced over the legs, a balanced spinal core, the arm structure balanced over the torso, and finally the skull balanced atop the spine. Each of these central points of balance is represented by a grey dot. Notice that these dots line up vertically to create a plumb line in the illustration. When our points of balance do not line up vertically, patterns of tension develop, such as those depicted in figure 18.2 on page 58.

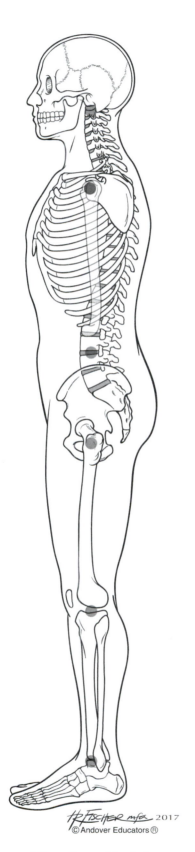

5.2 outline with skeleton

4. Take time to experience each of the major points of balance in your own skeleton. Notice that these points are all centrally located along the core of your body. Use your fingers to palpate your bones and locate your joints. Check with your kinesthetic sense to see if your muscles around each area are tense or free when you are sitting and standing.

    -Ankles
    -Knees
    -Hip joints
    -Lumbar spine
    -Humero-scapular joints, where your upper arm meets your torso
    -Atlanto-occipital joint, where your skull and spine meet

Even after all of these points are aligned and centered, it may be difficult to believe that you are balanced. Very often, singers who strive to have "good posture" use muscular effort to pull themselves up and back. True alignment may feel quite a bit more forward than those postural habits but more poised than a slumped posture.

5. Body Mapping is a different journey for each person. Your drawing will provide you with a few ideas about where to start. Give some attention each day to a map you wish to correct: look at anatomical illustrations or models, move the area you are mapping in new ways and pay attention to your whole body through multiple senses. As your map improves, so will your alignment and movement. Once that map is accurate and adequate, move on to the next one.

See the Appendix for additional resources to help you continue refining your body maps.

VI. Inclusive or Exclusive - Attention and Awareness

Inclusive Attention: For singers to be in top form, we must utilize inclusive attention. When doing so, we allow our focus to flow easily from one point to another within a wider field of awareness that encompasses all the senses, including kinesthesia. Look at a picture of a favorite musician, actor or athlete and imagine what is in his or her awareness at that moment. What is the primary focus? Secondary? Background? I love to show students a photo of Beverly Sills singing in a 1979 television show (see appendix). We imagine that in the background of

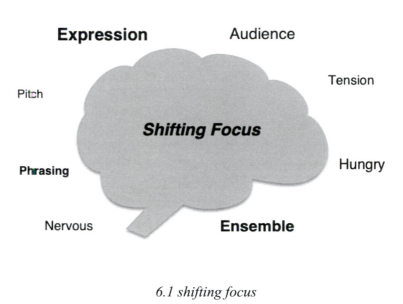

6.1 shifting focus

her consciousness is the feel of her costume and the lights on her face, the cameras and the scenic backdrop. Secondary information might include her physical movements, the sound of the orchestra, gestures of the conductor and the melody she is singing. She is able to give attention to the conductor or her pitch as needed without losing awareness of the music, her surroundings or herself. Within that larger field, her central focus is surely on the meaning of the phrase she is singing to the Muppet in front of her!

Exclusive Attention: Many of us are proud of our ability to concentrate, focusing our attention on one task or object while excluding all other input. You have probably had the experience of typing something on your computer, only to realize that the kitchen timer has been ringing for some time without your noticing. That is classic concentration! The ability to concentrate may be seen as highly desirable in some environments. For a musician, though, concentration can be devastating. Can you imagine performing as a soloist with an orchestra without easily being able to notice the conductor's gestures, the pitch of the violins, your musical score and artistic impulses?

Serial Concentration: When "concentrators" first start working to cultivate inclusive awareness, they often fall into the trap of serial concentration. In this state, attention shifts rapidly from one single point of focus to another. For example, when performing with a band a singer might concentrate first on the opening guitar chords to get a starting pitch, then count beats of the introduction, think about taking a breath, remember the first word, relax the shoulder that is tensing and so on, but remain completely unaware of the audience until they begin to applaud. While concentrating on one element of a song, this singer's attention will be pulled to another element when a problem arises, leading to a feeling of continually putting out fires. Serial concentration is even more exhausting than plain old concentration.

Let's use a flashlight analogy to illustrate the difference between these three types of attention. Imagine you are in a dark room with a flashlight and an elephant.

1. Inclusive attention: the flashlight has a soft focus with a bright center to the beam. You can aim that bright center at the elephant's eye, then trunk, then tail without losing sight of the rest of the elephant. The flashlight, which represents your awareness, will gently illuminate the whole elephant while picking out areas of interest with the bright center, which represents your focus.

2. Concentration: the flashlight has only a laser-like bright center without a soft focus. You can see only the elephant's eye in the bright center of the beam while the rest of the body remains in darkness.

3. Serial concentration: you can move the bright center from place to place, looking first at the elephant's eye, but then perhaps having trouble finding a knee or tusk in the darkness when you are ready to shift focus.

Sense

1. What is in your awareness right now? Are you concentrating on the words in front of you? Do you have a broader field of attention that includes sounds and movement around you, the comfortable (or uncomfortable) chair you are sitting in, the feel of the book in your hands? Are you aware of the taste or scent of the cup of tea you are sipping or the chips you are eating? Are you hungry or tired? Feeling energized or overwhelmed? Are you easily able to shift your primary focus from the book to your hand to the room without losing awareness of the rest of this sensory information?

2. Take a moment to pause. Become aware of your body, the movement of breathing, your emotions and the space around you. Allow your eyes to be soft and your body to be comfortable. How does that feel? If inclusive awareness is a new experience for you, it may seem a bit overwhelming. You may be concerned about what you will *do* with all that input. Not to worry, you don't have to do anything with the information. Just allow it to be there. Shutting the information out of your awareness takes effort. Allowing inclusive awareness is less effortful, but it may take some time to get used to it.

3. Find times throughout the day when you can practice inclusive attention. I don't recommend experimenting with it while driving or performing, but rather while you are washing your hands, walking to the bus or practicing a favorite song. Gradually you will find your field of attention widening throughout the day, in practice and performance, when biking or driving, and maybe even while working on the computer!

Sing

1. Sing a favorite song and allow your focus to shift after every few phrases. Use the statements below for guidance.

> I am aware of my voice.
> I am aware of my body moving.
> I am aware of my surroundings.
> I am aware of my thoughts.
> I am aware of my emotions.
> I am kinesthetically and emotionally aware.
> I am visually and aurally aware.
> I am aware of my self and my surroundings.

2. Sing another familiar song, and experiment with shifting your central focus while allowing yourself to remain inclusively aware. You might first focus on your dynamics, then your alignment, the objects in front of you, the space behind you, the movement of your ribs, the feeling of your feet on the floor, tactile sensations in your mouth and so on. Remember, all the sensory information is already flowing in to your brain. You simply need to recognize that it is there and choose how to organize it!

VII. Perfectly Poised - Your Head and Neck

Take a moment to visualize the place where your skull and spine meet. Where is the weight of your head delivered to your spine? When asked to find this joint, most people point to the back of the neck. In reality, the atlanto-occipital (A/O) joint is right between the ears, under the center of the base of the skull. After reading "Finding Balance" you know that the skull is poised upon the very top of the spine. When the head is pulled back or forward rather than being centered over the spine, this imbalance interferes with easy, efficient movement through the whole body.

In figure 7.1 you can see that the top vertebra of the spine, called the atlas, is right under the center of the skull. In figure 7.2 we see the atlas at the level of the earlobe, centered under the base of the skull. Notice that the atlas is quite broad, nearly as wide as the base of the skull. This strong top vertebra bears the weight of the head and delivers it to the rest of the spine through the springy spinal disks and bony vertebrae below.

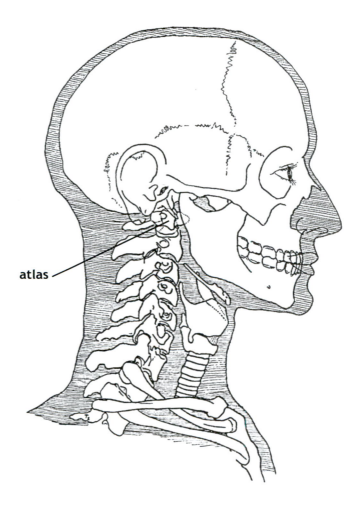

atlas

7.1 the skull, cervical spine and trachea

When the skull is aligned over the spine, the larger neck and back muscles relax. Look at figure 7.3 and notice how many neck muscles there are and how long they are. These muscles are not just in the back, but also in the front and sides of the neck, all around the throat. Freeing these larger muscles frees the voice and allows muscles nestled right up along the spine to automatically and continually find balance and buoyancy.

Once the skull and spine are aligned, neck muscles are available for their primary job, which is movement! Singers with tense neck muscles have difficulty playing a character convincingly. A tight neck won't allow Susannah to look up at the stars as she sings "Ain't it a pretty night?" Neck tension also makes it hard to move your head to see your band mates or conductor, interfering with ensemble. Singers with free neck muscles have graceful head and arm movement available to them. Their laryngeal and pharyngeal muscles are not compressed by surrounding neck muscles. As constriction is released, breathing improves. Free your neck to liberate your voice and body!

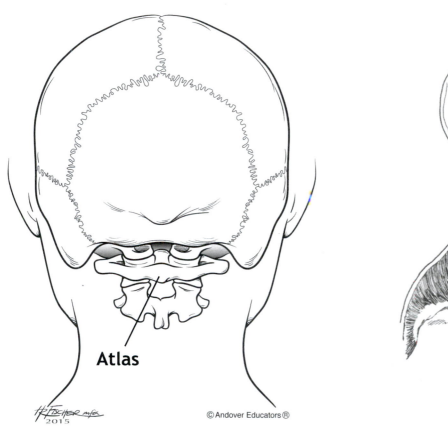

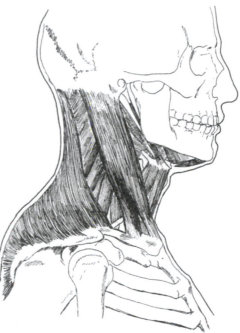

7.2 posterior view of A-O and atlas-axis joints   *7.3 neck muscles*

Sense

1. Put the tips of your index fingers on your earlobes and point the fingers straight across at one another. Refer to figure 7.2 and notice that you are pointing right at your A/O joint, where the weight of your head is delivered to your spine. Strong layers of connective tissue hold the bones together firmly but flexibly, allowing rocking and tipping of the curved skull on the concave surface of the atlas.

2. While pointing at the A/O joint, nod your head gently and notice what you feel. The tissues surrounding the A/O joint are rich in kinesthetic sense receptors, which send your brain information about how your atlas is moving in relationship to your skull and the rest of your spine. A smaller movement will be more localized around the A/O joint, while a larger motion will involve more of the spine and neck muscles. Try out both and feel the difference.

3. Some people can feel the outer edge of the wide atlas by palpating the neck just behind the jaw near the earlobes. Use figures 7.1 and 7.2 as guides as you gently search for your atlas. Whether or not you can feel the tips of your atlas with your fingertips, simply exploring this area will help clarify your body map.

Sing

Imagery is a powerful tool, but sometimes it leads us to adopt harmful habits. Singers are often asked to imagine that they are suspended from a string at the top of their head, like a puppet. This instruction is offered with the best of intentions by a teacher or conductor who wants the singer to release neck tension. Unfortunately, it can lead us to contract muscles in the front of the neck, tuck the chin and artificially straighten the spine. As a result, breathing and tone are compromised as the neck and back tense.

1. Stand as though you are a puppet suspended from a string. Notice any tension in your neck, back, abdomen, legs or elsewhere. Sing a few easy scales, noticing how you feel and sound. How is your breathing?

2. Now cut your puppet string! Rather than using muscles to "hold yourself up," allow the strong bones of your skeleton to deliver your weight to the ground. When your skeleton is balanced, the bones deliver your weight downward easily, freeing your muscles of extra work. Sing some more scales. Experiment with balance, letting your weight be delivered downward by your bones. How does that feel and sound? Has your breathing changed?

3. Sit comfortably on the front of your chair and find balance at your A/O joint. When your skull is centered over the spine, your neck muscles will be free of the chore of "holding up" your head. You may feel buoyant or even a bit like a bobble-head doll as your head moves slightly to continually return to balance.

4. Now slowly tilt your head back to look up and notice what is happening to the muscles in the front of your neck and torso. They are contracting because the weight of your head is no longer balanced over your spine. As you tip your head forward to look down, you may feel the muscles in the back of your neck and torso contract as your head moves forward of balance. If you released those muscles, your head would drop forward. Gently bring your head to balance over your spine, allowing the large outer muscles of your neck to relax as automatic postural reflexes take over.

5. Repeat this exercise, singing a long, comfortable "ah." How does singing feel and sound when you are balanced and buoyant? When your head is pulled back or forward?

VIII. Central Core - Your Spine

At the very core of the body is the spine, comprised of twenty-four vertebrae, twenty-three intervertebral discs and the spinal cord. The structure of the spine allows a wide variety of movement, including the amazing feat of walking upright. We may not think much about the spine, but it plays a central role in singing. The spine provides crucial support for the diaphragm and other breathing muscles, allows easy rib movement, and coordinates integrated movement through the whole body. Our singing structures are all nestled along the spine, from the pelvic floor to the soft palate. Those little bumps you feel along the center of your back are just the tip of the iceberg, though!

The spine is much larger and more elegant than most people imagine. The atlas vertebra at the top of the spine is right between the ear lobes. The tailbone at the base is near the level of your hip joints. From left to right, figure 8.1 shows three views of the spine: front, back and side. Can you tell which way the spine is facing in the side view? The front of the spine is facing left, so the bumpy processes you see closer to the margin are the ones you can feel when you run your fingers along your back. Notice the small spaces between those processes and the larger vertebral bodies: that is where nerves emerge from the spinal cord. The side view shows how deep the vertebrae are and how curvy the spine is. The curves in the spine are important to healthy spinal function, providing strength and resilience. Standing up "straight" is neither natural nor necessary.

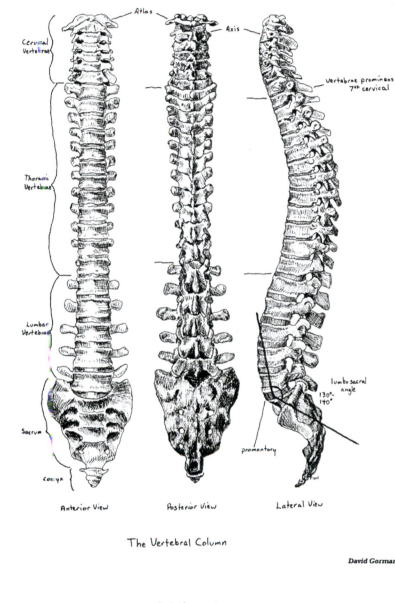

The Vertebral Column

David Gorman

8.1 the spine

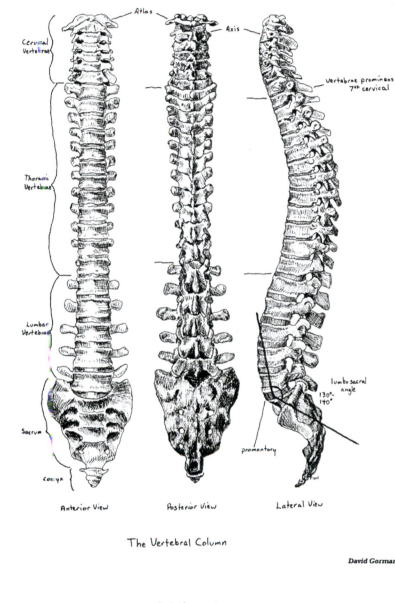

22

Many singers are "back oriented." They believe that the spine is at the very back of the torso and so try to put their weight there. However, you can see that the discs are cushioning the strong vertebral bodies in the front of the spine. Compare the anterior and posterior views. You will see that the spine is designed to carry weight in front. The bony processes at the back and sides are for attachment to muscles, ligaments and ribs.

If you look closely at figures 8.1 and 8.2, you will see that weight is not delivered directly from bone to bone. The discs of the spine help transfer weight in an elastic manner, protecting the vertebrae from compression and shock while allowing flexibility and strength in movement. These tough, springy cartilaginous discs are one example of the importance of connective tissue in healthy movement. Connective tissue is elastic and strong. It forms our tendons, cartilage and fascia and helps shape all the structures of the body, from bones to individual cells. A comprehensive network of connective tissue organizes the diverse elements of our bodies into a fluid, cohesive whole. When we are poised and breathing well, the spine is continually moving in relationship with the other structures of breathing within the context of the whole body. Look for more information about integrated movement and connective tissue in Chapter 16 and the Appendix.

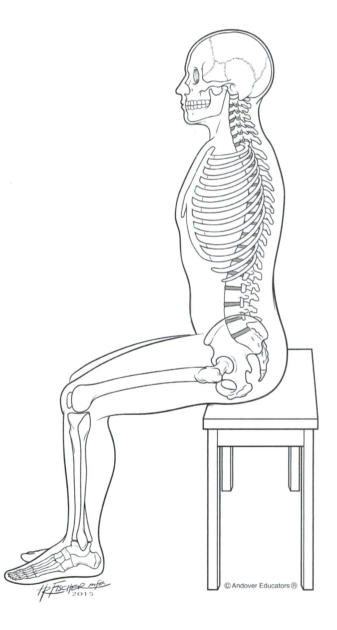

Sense

Many people use the term "core" to refer to large muscle groups in the abdomen but lose sight of the skeletal core. It is important to map the size and shape of your spine as well as its many functions. The spine delivers the weight of your body—via the pelvis, legs and connective tissue—to the chair or floor below you. This leaves your muscles free to take care of movement!

1. To find the weight-bearing front portion of your lumbar spine, use Figure 8.2 as a guide. Palpate the sides of your torso above your hip joints to find the top of your pelvis, or iliac crest. Find the highest area of your iliac crest on each side—it will be about where the side seams are on your pants or shirt.

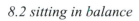

8.2 sitting in balance

2. From that place, point straight across toward the center of your body. You should be pointing to an area behind your navel, several inches in front of the curve in your lower back, right at the vertebral bodies of your lumbar spine. When you are well-balanced and using your spine effectively, weight travels down through the front of the spine, through the area you are pointing to, and onward to the pelvis. From there it is delivered to your chair, or to the ground through your legs and feet.

3. Your strong, flexible intervertebral discs and individual vertebrae allow your spine to move in a variety of ways. Sit comfortably on a chair and move your spine in as many ways as you can while paying close attention to the kinesthetic information your nerves are sending to your brain. Bend, spiral, arch and extend the full length of your spine. Are certain areas of your spine more mobile than others? Is it easier for you to move in one direction than another? Can you feel your movement accurately using your kinesthetic awareness? Notice how your whole body participates in this movement.

Paper the World With the Truth

By now you have probably identified a few errors in your map of the spine. This activity will prompt you to become aware of your body many times each day, with special attention to areas you are working on.

1. Make ten full-page copies of figure 8.2[1]. Color each one differently, highlighting body maps you would like to correct. Perhaps in one you would like to emphasize the relationship of the spine and skull. In another you could color the weight-bearing front of the spine. A third might have arrows showing where your weight is delivered by your bones to the bench and floor. And so on.

2. After coloring, post the pages in places you will see them throughout the day—the refrigerator door, bathroom mirror, music folder, etcetera. Each time you see a picture it will give your brain a little bit of anatomical truth and help refine your body maps. You might use it as a reminder to move attentively, further accelerating the process of Body Mapping! Choose a new image each week as you progress.

---

[1]Please don't share the image.

IX. Balance and Support - Your Pelvis

Whether sitting or standing, the pelvis provides sturdy support for the structures of breathing. The pelvis is a ring-shaped group of three bones: the sacrum and two wing-shaped pelvic bones. These bones articulate at joints, allowing subtle mobility of the pelvic "ring."

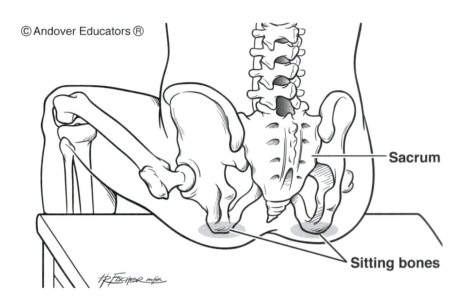

9.1 the pelvis in context

The pelvis is connected to the thorax above by the lumbar vertebrae. The bottom of the pelvis forms two curved rockers, often called the "sitting bones." On the outer surface of the pelvic bones, the legs attach to the torso at the hip joints. These joints are right at the mid-point of the body, the same distance from the feet as from the top of the head.

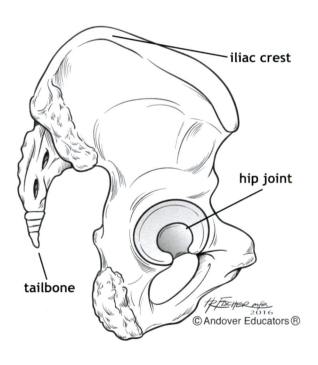

9.2 lateral male pelvis

Weight is delivered downward through the spinal vertebrae and discs to the pelvis. When we are seated, the sitting bones deliver that weight to our chair. When we are standing, the weight is delivered through the hip joints to the leg bones for delivery to the floor. Study the illustrations to become familiar with the 3-dimensional shape of the pelvis.

The pelvis is important to breathing in many ways. It serves as a container for the organs of the lower abdomen and pelvis. Its position affects the shape of all the organs, including the lungs. Many respiratory muscles, including the diaphragm, are attached to the lumbar vertebrae, which link the pelvis and thoracic skeleton. Any imbalance in the pelvis will negatively influence the spine and related muscles. Finding pelvic balance is crucial to releasing excess work in the back, abdominal and leg muscles.

An important area often overlooked by singers is the pelvic floor. This sling-like network of muscles attaches to the very base of the spine and all around the inner edges of the pelvis, as seen in figure 17.1. Pelvic muscles support and move our abdominal and pelvic organs. Figure 9.3 shows how the diaphragm's action affects the pelvic floor. Healthy, free pelvic muscles yield to downward pressure of the organs caused by movement of the diaphragm during inhalation. They then spring back to neutral during exhalation. This elastic recoil effortlessly energizes vocal tone. It is coordinated with the rebound of the abdominal muscles and with spinal mobility, which we will explore in greater detail in Chapters 13 and 16. Pelvic tension interferes with this supportive elasticity and can cause imbalance through the body, from the soles of the feet to the larynx, tongue and palate.

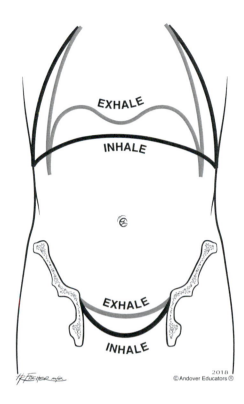

9.3 the diaphragm and pelvic floor

Sense

Use the illustrations as a guide while you explore the structure of your pelvis.

1. Seated comfortably, find your iliac crests with your fingertips - this ridge forms the top of your pelvis on each side. Notice how tall your pelvis is, from your sitting bones on the chair to the iliac crests. Follow the upper edge of your pelvic bones around to your back and then down towards your tailbone. Feel the broad, flattened sacrum that forms the back of your pelvis and the lowest part of your spine. Follow the top of your pelvic bones around toward the front. You will be able to palpate the iliac crest and pubic crest, but much of the front of the pelvis is nestled within layers of muscle and connective tissue.

2. Look at the illustrations as you use your kinesthetic sense and fingertips to find the true location of your hip joints. Many people think the legs attach to the body at the top of the iliac crests or at the bottom of the pelvis, but the hip joints are actually about midway between those points on either side of the pelvis. You will not be able to palpate your hip joints directly, but you can locate the joints through the sensation of movement.

3. Sit on a piano bench or other firm, level surface with your feet on the floor and knees about level with your hip joints. Notice how your sitting bones are delivering the weight of your upper body to the seat. Your legs are to the sides of your pelvis, not under it.

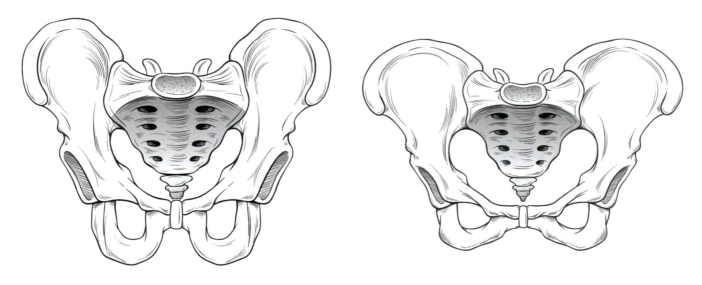

9.4 anterior male pelvis   *9.5 anterior female pelvis*

4. Rock forward and back slightly and feel the shifting contact of your sitting bones with the seat. Your legs can remain relatively still as your pelvis rocks. As your sitting bones move on the seat, notice their shape. Are they curved? Are there any places that are flat or pointed? Can you feel that the sitting bones are closer to one another in the front and farther apart at the back? How far can you rock and still feel the sitting bones in contact with the seat?

5. Tune in to the muscles of the pelvic floor with this exercise from *The Breathing Book for Flute* by Amy Likar:

   1. Fold a washcloth or hand towel and place it on the corner of a firm chair or piano bench. Sit on the washcloth and you will feel that it puts some pressure on your pelvic floor between your sitting bones. Take the time to cycle through an exhalation, rest, inhalation and transition to exhalation. Notice the mobility of the musculature of your pelvic floor into the washcloth as you go through a few breath cycles.

   2. Then gently tense the muscles of your pelvic floor, as if you were clenching to keep from going to the bathroom. Go through a few more breath cycles. Notice the effect that this clenching has on the mobility of your pelvic floor, in addition to the mobility of your ribs and the amount of air you can inhale. Then release that tension, and go through a few more breath cycles. Hopefully you notice that when you release this tension, it is easier to breathe and get the amount of air you need. Notice that when you have ease and mobility in the muscles of your pelvic floor and gluteal muscles, there is more of a sense of ease in your arms.

Sing

Experiment with seated pelvic balance as you sing a familiar song or warmup.

1. As you rock back, do you notice work in the front of your torso and neck? How does this position affect your breathing and your singing? Are you able to move your jaw and tongue freely?

2. How does your singing change when you are rocked forward? Do you feel more weight through your feet and legs? Is breathing easy or difficult?

3. Notice how your whole body feels and how your voice sounds when you are balanced over your sitting bones. Are your back and abdominal muscles released? Is your neck free? Is breathing easy? Are your words and tone clear?

4. How does balanced singing compare to singing forward or back of balance? Once we have found balance we can return to it again and again. When staging or gesture requires you to sing forward or back of balance, that movement can be achieved by starting at balance and making good use of the contact with the front or back portions of your sitting bones on the seat or your feet on the floor.

5. Continue to explore moving through balance as you sing. Allow your weight to be delivered to your seat through your sitting bones. Seek balance and freedom in your torso and neck as you move away from and back to balance on your seat.

X. Weight Delivery - Your Legs

Many singers wonder what to do with their legs when they are performing. "Should I have my feet in a certain position?" "Why are my knees locked?" These questions and many more can be addressed simply by getting to know your legs from the ground up.

Feet are dynamic, mobile structures. Each foot is made up of 26 bones and 31 joints, providing a great deal of flexibility and strength. The bones are arranged in arching formations that direct the weight of your body downward and outward for delivery to the ground. In figures 10.1, 10.2 and 5.2 notice that the ankle is at the very

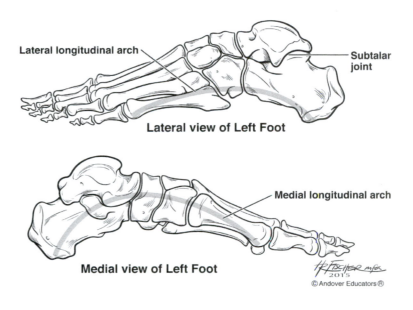

10.1 lateral and medial views of the left foot

top of the foot. The ankle is not directly over the heel, as so many singers imagine. In standing, each foot acts as a springy tripod, ideally delivering the body's weight to the ground at the heel and the inner and outer ball of the foot. In singers who have mapped the feet as flat, blocky structures, the resulting tension affects the whole body. Breathing, singing and moving all benefit from exploring the truth.

The knee joints transfer weight between the upper and lower legs. They also bend, balance and lock. As figure 10.3 shows, the knee joint is quite large. Many singers mistakenly equate the kneecap with the knee joint. The joint is actually located behind and slightly below the kneecap. Locked knees are a symptom of a body that is off balance due to mismapping of the skeletal structure. Improving overall skeletal balance reduces strain on the knee and hip joints, frees the neck and back muscles and liberates the breath.

Because of their shape and the numerous muscles surrounding them, the hip joints are strong and flexible. Notice in figure 10.4 that the hip joints are on the outside of the pelvis at the sides. Whether seated or standing, the pelvis rests between the upper leg bones, not on top of them. Weight from the torso above is

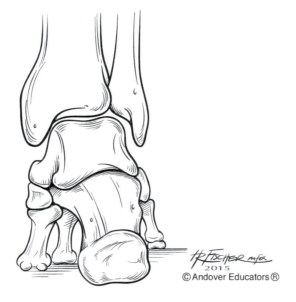

10.2 posterior heel (right foot)

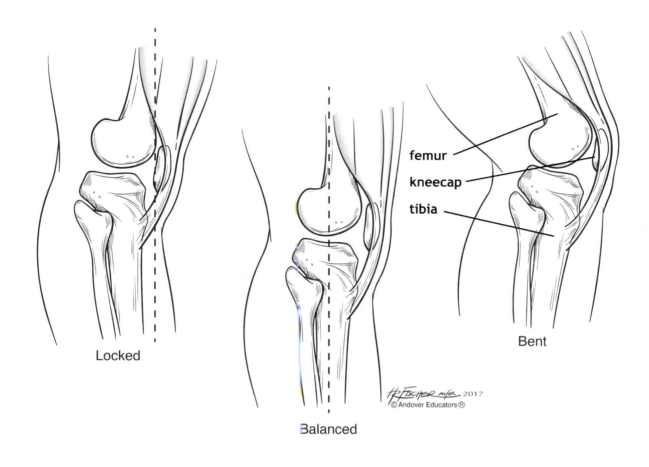

femur
kneecap
tibia

Locked

Balanced

Bent

10.3 lateral right knee

delivered down and out through the strong bones of the pelvis to the leg bones when standing. If you turn back to figure 5.2 again, you will see that the hip joints are in the middle of the body, where the upper and lower halves of the body articulate. The middle of the body is here, not at the waist as so many have mapped it to their detriment. Finding balance here, at the center of the skeleton, allows greater ease and fluidity through the whole body.

Sense

1. Sit on the front edge of a chair. Lift and lower one leg at a time, as though you are marching. Notice that your legs are on the outside of your pelvis and that they can move freely while your pelvis rests on the chair.

2. Explore your hip joints' range of motion: extend a leg to the side, make big circles with one foot, sway your knees from side to side, extend your legs forward and rock your feet side to side like windshield wipers, and so on. Can you feel movement in the muscles and connective tissues around your hip joints?

3. With both hands palpate the area around one of your knees. Run your hands along your femur (thigh bone) and notice where it widens just above the knee joint. Wrap your hands around this widest area of your femur to get a sense of how large it is. Now do the same with your tibia (shin bone). Study the illustrations to see how these two bones relate to one another.

4. Palpate your kneecap and note its relationship to the knee joint. Notice that when your leg is straight and relaxed you can actually move the kneecap from side to side with your fingers. The kneecap is not the knee joint!

5. Stand and notice how weight is delivered through your feet to the floor. Is more weight in one foot than the other? Do you feel more weight in the heels or the balls of your feet, or is it distributed evenly?

Sing

1. Once you are warmed up, stand as you usually do. Sing a familiar piece while giving special attention to your legs. Notice whether your leg muscles are tense or released, if your knees are locked, and what parts of your feet are delivering the most weight to the floor. How does your whole body feel?

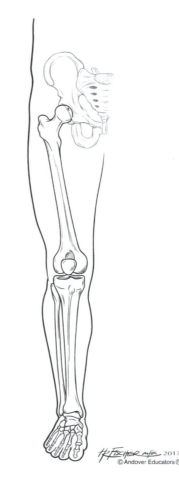

10.4 anterior view of the right leg

2. Explore each of these stances for a minute or two as you sing. Notice how your overall balance is affected by how you stand. Do you feel changes in your neck, torso, arms or legs? Does your breathing change along with your stance?

　　-Feet together, toes pointing forward
　　-Heels together, toes pointing outward
　　-Feet a few inches apart, most of your weight on one foot
　　-Most of your weight on your heels
　　-Most of your weight on the balls of your feet

3. Be sure you have space to move, then sing your piece again. Take a few steps backward as you sing, then stand still. Take a few steps forward. Repeat this process a few times. As you prepare to walk, especially backwards, do you find that you have to unlock your knee or hip joints to move? How does your overall balance feel in that "unlocked" moment? Notice how your breathing and singing change as you alternate standing and walking.

XI. Breathing Joints - Your Ribs and Spine

In preceding pages we have examined parts of the skeleton that provide the supportive framework for the structures and muscles of breathing. Here we explore the bony structure that is most directly involved in breathing, the thoracic skeleton. This structure is made up of the ribs, thoracic spine and sternum. It houses the lungs and heart and provides the skeletal framework for that workhorse of inhalation, the diaphragm.

Twelve pairs of ribs form most of the thoracic skeleton. In back, these ribs meet the spine at joints, as shown in figure 11.1. The neck of each rib articulates with the transverse process of the corresponding vertebra. The head of each rib articulates with the body of the corresponding vertebra and of the vertebra just above. Efficient breathing requires unfettered movement at each of these costo-vertebral joints.

In front, ten pairs of ribs are connected to the sternum by costal cartilages of varying lengths, seen in figure 11.2. The upper ribs are joined to the sternum by shorter cartilages, so the movement of these ribs during inhalation tends to be more forward and up. Increasingly longer cartilages allow the middle and lower ribs a greater sideways range of motion. Because they are not attached to the sternum at all, the bottom two pairs of ribs, called "floating ribs," can move up and back as we inhale.

When the body is aligned and free of tension, the ribs, sternum and spine move with every

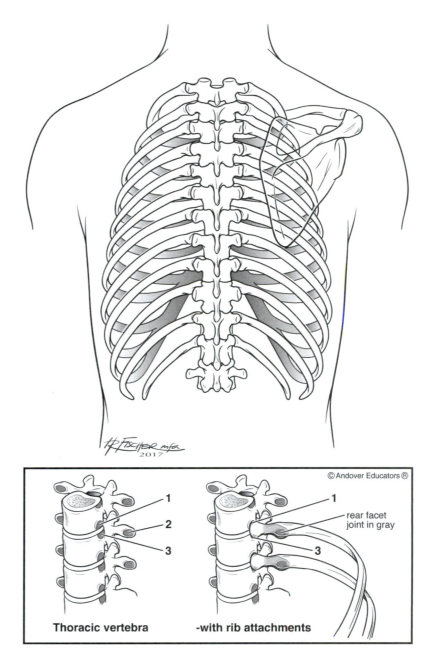

11.1 the ribs and spine

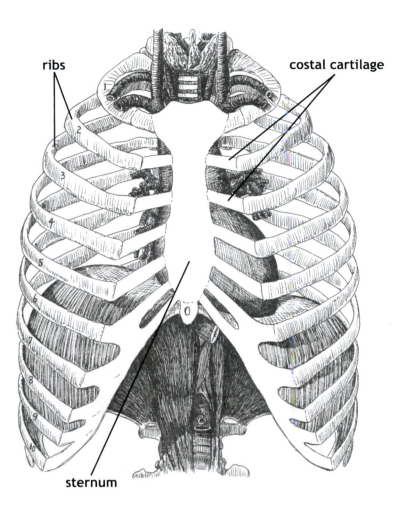

ribs

costal cartilage

sternum

11.2 the ribs, costal cartilage, and sternum

breath. Kinesthetic sense receptors send information to the brain about this movement. This kinesthetic feedback provides important information about how far the ribs have moved, how much air was taken in and how much remains in the lungs as we speak or sing.

Despite the implications of its common name, the rib "cage" is very flexible. The thin, curved rib bones are quite elastic and can be bent and twisted to varying degrees. The costal cartilages connecting the top ten pairs of ribs to the sternum are even more elastic than the ribs themselves. Finally, there are more than 80 joints in the thoracic skeleton. These combined elements provide an innate flexibility that allows us to move our ribs in an infinite variety of ways and tailor each breath according to our artistic choices.

Finding and optimizing flexibility in the ribs is essential to good breathing. In singers who have mapped the ribs as a rigid cage without joints, breathing is compromised by limited movement of the ribs, spine and diaphragm. Notice where your maps differ from reality. Do you think of the ribs as having moving joints with the spine in back? Have you mapped a square, rigid "cage" or a flexible, beehive-shaped structure? Mapping the thoracic skeleton accurately gives singers access to easy and efficient movement of the ribs. Each elegant breath oxygenates the blood and supports expressive, buoyant vocal tone.

Sense

1. Figure 11.2 shows the costal cartilages (white) that attach the bony ribs (gray) to the sternum in front. Press firmly on your ribs to compare the springiness of the cartilage in front with the firmer rib bones at your sides and back.

2. Sit in a chair and use your hands and fingertips to feel your ribs as you move your torso. Notice that your ribs may be closer together or further apart as you change position. Tune in to your kinesthetic sense to feel these movements from the inside, too.

    -arch your back like a cat
    -extend your spine to look at the ceiling above you
    -twist slowly to look behind you
    -bend to one side and then the other

3. Use your hands and fingertips to feel the movement of your ribs as you breathe. You may also watch your movements in a mirror or on a video. Experiment with smaller and larger breaths as well as faster and slower breathing. Explore your rib movement at the sides as well as in front and in back, all the way from the lowest floating ribs to the highest ribs at the level of your collarbones. Each pair of ribs moves on a slightly different trajectory than their neighboring ribs. Does the kinesthetic information from your moving thoracic skeleton match what your hands are feeling and what you see in the mirror?

Sing

As you sing a favorite song, use your tactile sense to notice the movement of your ribs. Also observe your movement from all angles with mirrors or video. Here are some things to notice:

1. As you inhale, do you notice movement in your thorax, abdomen, or both?

2. Does your sternum swing up and forward, away from your thoracic spine?

3. Do your ribs swing out to the side, widening your torso?

4. Do your ribs descend fully to neutral as you sing each phrase, allowing you to take in fresh air with the next inhalation?

5. Is your movement proportional to the phrases you are singing? In other words, do you move a little bit to take in a small amount of air for shorter phrases and move more to take in more air for longer phrases?

6. Does the information from your kinesthetic sense match what you see in the mirror or video?

7. Do you hear changes in your sound that coincide with changes in your movement?

You may find that your kinesthetic sense is not giving you accurate information about your movement. If so, revisit these exercises daily until you are able to feel your movement accurately.

XII. Muscles Move Bones - Rib Mobility

Most of us understand that when we raise our arm, muscles are doing the work of moving the bones. We can choose to release the muscular work quickly and allow the arm to drop, or we can release the work slowly and lower the arm gracefully. The same principle applies to rib movement during breathing. Muscles swing the ribs up and out, causing the thoracic space to increase and air to flow into the lungs. It is not possible for the delicate tissue of the lungs to move the ribs, or for the air itself to push the ribs outward. Muscles move bones; air does not.

While the diaphragm is the primary muscle of inhalation, accessory muscles play an important role in refining and managing the singer's breath. Three categories of muscles can move the ribs during inhalation: muscles that lift the ribs from the thoracic spine, from the upper arm structure, and from the head and neck. Our choices about breathing affect which of those muscles will be called upon to work. For singers, it is usually best to avoid the latter group, leaving the head and neck free for other vocal tasks. Let's look at examples from the first two groups.

In figure 12.1 the levator costarum muscles are shown in dark gray. These muscles originate at each of the vertebral processes of the thoracic spine. They descend laterally to insert on the surface of the first or second rib below. When the spine is balanced and stable, contraction of this group of muscles moves the ribs at the costo-vertebral joints, levering them up and away from the spine. This movement increases the diameter of the thoracic cavity, causing air to flow into the lungs.

You may have noticed that intercostal muscles appear in figure

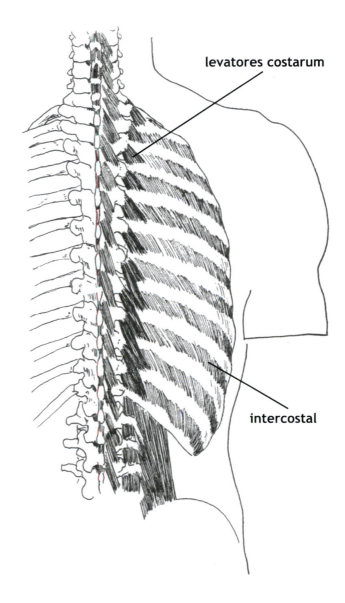

levatores costarum

intercostal

12.1 levator costarum and intercostal muscles

12.1. Many pedagogical texts cite the intercostals as a primary respiratory group. However, while most current sources agree that the intercostals help stabilize the thoracic skeleton, their exact respiratory function is controversial. Luckily, there is no need to micro-manage specific muscles. A basic understanding of the rib muscles, coupled with clear movement intentions, empowers a singer to begin fine-tuning the breath.

The serratus anterior, seen in figure 12.2, spreads across the side of the rib cage. The fibers of this muscle group run over the ribs and beneath the shoulder blade. They originate on the underside of the shoulder blade and attach to ribs 1 through 10. When the serratus anterior contracts, the lower five attachments pull back on the ribs. This action causes the ribs to swing up and out, increasing thoracic diameter. Gradual release of this muscle helps slow the pace of exhalation. The serratus anterior is one of the most powerful accessory muscles of inhalation. It is also a large arm-moving muscle, so imbalance in the arm structure can interfere with its effectiveness.

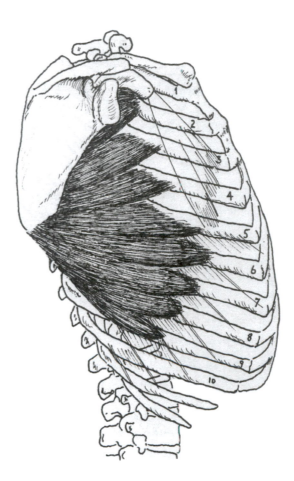

12.2 serratus anterior muscles

Muscles of inhalation can be activated in various combinations to meet different needs. Which muscles are engaged determines whether movement is emphasized in the thorax or abdomen, front, back or sides of the torso, or evenly distributed. For example, a singer who is tap dancing might favor muscles that will bring about a more lateral mid-torso inhalation, leaving abdominal muscles free to engage in leg movement. While standing still, that same singer may choose to breathe with more abdominal movement. Singers must be wary, though, of taking any movement choice to extremes, such as rigidly holding the ribs in an elevated position at all times. This type of imbalanced approach limits the amount of air available for singing and for oxygenating the blood. It can result in dizziness, muscle fatigue or injury, and impairs the whole-body micro-movement of breathing, causing the singer to appear and feel stiff.

Refined use of rib muscles allows singers to manage the breath skillfully and artistically. During inhalation we may use these muscles to move the ribs a little or a lot, faster or slower. Choosing to release these muscles quickly or more slowly gives singers the opportunity to fine-tune exhalation to meet the demands of each phrase. The most skillful singers use rib muscles in cooperation with the diaphragm to take in just the right amount of air for each phrase, then gradually and fully exhale so that the lungs are ready to take in fresh air when the phrase ends.

Sense

1. Sit comfortably balanced in front of a mirror. You may find it helpful to tie a Thera-band or knit scarf around your ribs to create tactile feedback. Take a breath and sigh, releasing your breath quickly. Repeat this sigh a few times, feeling and watching the movement of your ribs. As you inhale, your rib-moving muscles can swing your ribs up and out, causing your torso to widen and deepen. When you sigh, feel the muscles release and drop the ribs quickly. If you notice any tension in your neck or abdominal muscles during this activity, allow those muscles to soften and release. Now inhale, but pause before exhaling, allowing your vocal folds to remain open. Exhale slowly and silently, allowing your rib-moving muscles to release gradually, slowly lowering your ribs to their resting state. How long can you extend this silent exhalation by slowing the descent of your ribs?

2. Inspired by a similar practice in *The Anatomy of Breathing* by Blandine Calais-Germaine, the following exercises cultivate awareness of breathing movement in the back and sides of the torso:

   A. Sit on a chair or bench with your feet on a low stool or pile of books to elevate your knees. Roll forward so your abdomen rests on your thighs or a pillow and your spine is rounded. Have a partner place his or her hands on your low back, between your ribs and pelvis. Remaining aware of your whole body, focus your attention on the area where your partner's hands rest, gradually increasing movement in that area. You may think of "breathing to" your partner's hands, but remember that you are moving the air, the air is not moving you. Your diaphragm creates much of this breathing movement in your lower ribs and back.

   B. After a minute or two focusing on the lower back, your partner's hands can move up to your middle back, just under your shoulder blades. Now notice the movement of your middle and lower ribs. You may feel your torso widening as the middle ribs swing up and out to the side. As your ribs move through their full excursion, notice how much air you take in. Allow the ribs to return fully to neutral as you exhale. It is not necessary to micro-manage the rib muscles. Simply ask for more movement, then notice the degree and quality of movement. If you notice excess effort or tension in your neck or back, take a moment to release it, then continue your exploration.

   C. Placing your partner's hands between the shoulder blades will call upon other accessory muscles to move the less-mobile upper ribs. Allow the range of motion to gradually increase. You may notice that your sternum swings forward and up with the ribs as you inhale, away from your thoracic spine. As you exhale, allow your ribs, spine and sternum to return fully to their resting position.

XIII. Elastic Recoil - Your Abdominal Muscles

The large, strong abdominal muscles play an important role in breath management. When functioning optimally, they allow us to create a stunning variety of vocal sounds. When misunderstood and misused, they are capable of disrupting vocal tone or damaging and even destroying voices. One way to maintain a healthy voice is to be sure that your map of the abdominal muscles is accurate and adequate in terms of size, structure *and* function.

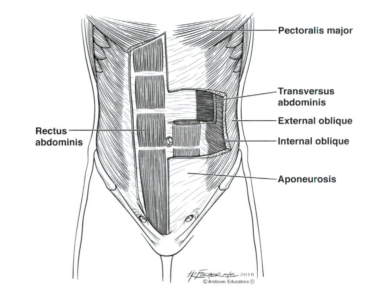

13.1 abdominal muscles

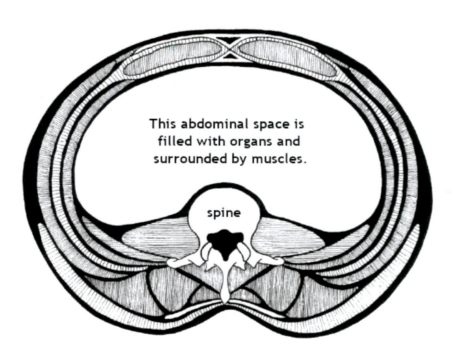

13.2 abdominal space cross section

There are four layers of abdominal muscles, seen in figure 13.1. As a group, these muscles attach to points as low as the pelvis and as high as the fifth rib. Abdominal muscles are not confined to the front of the body, but span the sides and back of the torso, too. They have attachments all along the lumbar spine and around the circumference of the ribs and pelvis. Figure 13.2 shows the layers of abdominal muscles in cross section with the lumbar spine and deep back muscles, all of which surround the abdominal organs.

Abdominal muscles move and support the bones and organs of the torso. While the abdominal muscles can be isolated, during breathing they function as a group to support exhalation. Abdominals can increase the speed, force and degree of exhalation by moving the organs upward against the diaphragm and pulling down and in on the lower ribs. These actions decrease thoracic volume, increasing pressure on the lungs to promote exhalation. Gentle engagement of the abdominal muscles allows singers to extend and enhance exhalation as needed. However, the abdominal muscles do not necessarily have to contract during exhalation.

During inhalation the diaphragm presses down on the abdominal organs. As the organs slip and slide below the descending diaphragm, they put outward pressure on the cylinder of abdominal muscles. Free, flexible abdominal and pelvic muscles respond to this pressure by allowing the abdominal cylinder to expand in all directions. When inhalation is complete, the muscles then effortlessly spring back towards their resting state, encouraging the inward and upward flow of the organs, ascent of the diaphragm and outflow of breath. Free, springy abdominal muscles support free, flexible singing!

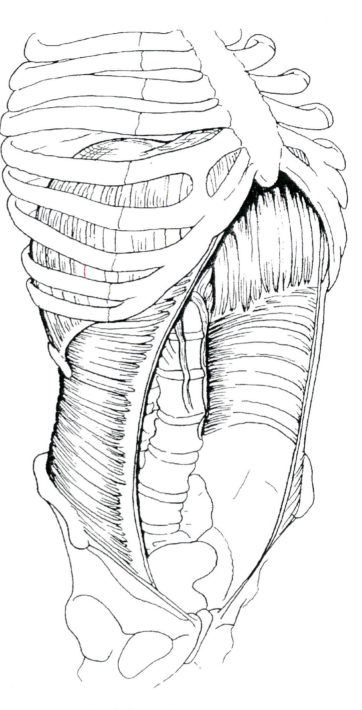

13.3 abdominal space cut-away

The vocal folds and other intrinsic muscles of the larynx are tiny in comparison with the abdominal muscles. During phonation, when the closed vocal folds vibrate in the breath stream, the actions of abdominal and laryngeal muscles are in opposition. When these muscle groups cooperate, air flow and sub-glottal pressure are flexible, responding easily to vocal and musical ideas. Excess work in one set of muscles will cause tension in the other, though. It takes care, skill and accurate body maps to enable these very different muscle groups to work together in dynamic equilibrium.

Sense

1. Using the illustrations as guides, palpate your abdominal muscles. Note how large they are as a group and how they relate to your ribs, spine and pelvis.

   A. The vertical fibers of the rectus abdominis extend from your fifth ribs down to the pubic crest of your pelvis.

   B. The diagonal fibers of the internal and external obliques create a criss-cross pattern all around your abdomen.

   C. The horizontal fibers of the transverse abdominals wrap around the sides of your abdomen and attach to your lumbar vertebrae in back. Under your ribs, transverse fibers intertwine with those of your diaphragm. From Blandine Calais-Germaine's *Anatomy of Breathing,* figure 13.3 illustrates beautifully the depth of the abdominal cavity, the central location of the large, strong lumbar spine and the relationship of the transverse abdominals to the diaphragm.

2. Breathe a few times while maintaining a skinny "waist," noticing any tension in your abdomen and throughout your body. Then release the idea of a waist, allowing your abdomen to widen and deepen naturally as you inhale. Notice how this change affects your breathing and your whole body.

3. Sit on a chair and roll your torso forward as far as you comfortably can. Place your feet on a raised surface or put a pillow on your lap so your abdomen is well-supported. This position limits the forward movement of your abdomen. Relax and breathe here for a few minutes, noticing movement in the sides and back of your torso. Can you distinguish between the sensation of movement at your costo-vertebral joints, where your ribs and spine meet, and the feeling of your abdominal muscles being stretched as you inhale?

4. Sitting comfortably balanced, take a breath and sigh. Notice the elasticity of your abdominal muscles effortlessly supporting the sigh. Repeat several times, extending the length of the sigh just a bit each time. At what point during the sigh do your abdominal muscles actively engage? Add voice to your sigh, again noticing the effortless elastic recoil of your abdominal muscles at the onset of sound.

5. If you are one of the many singers who think of "supporting" or "projecting" the voice with breath, consider your map of vocal sound. We must recognize that sound does not have mass and can not be propelled in any direction. Only then can over-active abdominal muscles release and respond easily to artistic impulses, as breath management replaces breath support.

Sing

1. Stand and find your best skeletal balance, allowing your back to be long and wide and your abdominal muscles to be free and responsive. Sing a favorite song, noticing how your abdominal muscles move and contribute to breathing.

2. Now take on your old, habitual stance as you sing the song again. Perhaps your knees are locked and your neck is overly straight. Maybe you are slouched and slumped. Notice how postural habits play into your breathing. Are your abdominal muscles too busy holding you upright to contribute easily to breathing? Are your ribs moving easily through their full range of motion, or are they compressed and held? Alternate these stances and experiment with others if you wish. Notice how each stance affects your abdominal muscles, breath, voice and mood.

XIV. Free Flow - Your Vocal Tract

Our breath courses through several passageways on its journey to and from the lungs. These spaces include the mouth, nose, pharynx and larynx, which form the vocal tract, and the trachea. How we perceive and utilize these structures may help or hinder our breathing. While mouth and throat muscles are active in gathering nourishment, the work of inhalation happens far from the head and neck. As the thoracic space expands and air flows into the body, we may simply "get out of the way" and allow the breath to flow freely. Unnecessary work in the muscles of the mouth, pharynx or larynx can restrict airflow and cause noisy breathing. Other than opening the vocal folds during inhalation, there is no other breathing work to be done here.

Confusion around the shared digestive and respiratory functions of the mouth and throat can lead to difficulty in breathing. One example of this confusion is mixing up the two "tubes" of the throat. The trachea, or air tube, is in the very front of the neck just below the larynx. Behind the larynx and trachea is the muscular esophagus, through which food and drink pass, just in front of the cervical spine. The esophagus flattens when empty, but the trachea is open and air-filled at all times. Singers with fantasies of projecting sound or breathing into the back of the throat may inadvertently activate the esophageal muscles, causing tension and noisy breathing.

Because it is a space surrounded by moving parts, the mouth can take on a great variety of shapes and sizes. Some movements of the singer's lips, cheeks, jaw, tongue and soft palate create vowels and consonants as well as influence timbre and dynamics. Other movements of these structures are more appropriate for chewing and swallowing. When teachers ask us not to "chew the words" or "swallow the tone," they are instructing us to use these muscles in ways that are meant for communication rather than for consumption.

Notice the size and shape of the tongue in figure 14.1. It is much

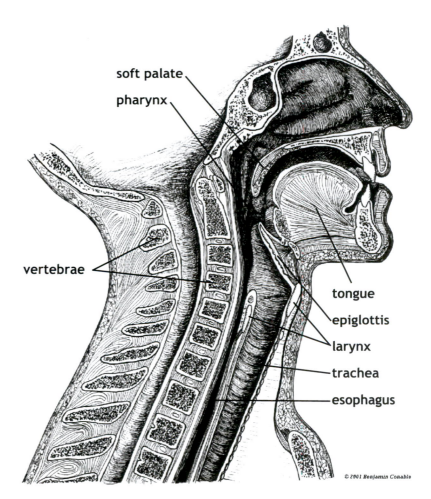

soft palate

pharynx

vertebrae

tongue

epiglottis

larynx

trachea

esophagus

© 2001 Benjamin Conable

14.1 the tongue, mouth and throat

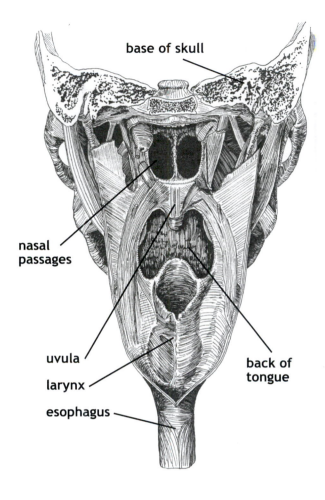

base of skull

nasal
passages

uvula

larynx

esophagus

back of
tongue

14.2 vocal tract from behind

larger than many singers imagine. In fact, the back of the tongue serves as the front of the upper throat. The tongue is comprised of eight muscle pairs, some shared with the soft palate and pharynx, which may be activated in various combinations.

A singer may choose to inhale through the mouth when a quick or large breath is required. Air taken in through the narrower, winding nasal passages is warmed, moistened and filtered as it passes through, which makes it preferable in many situations. Both the nasal and oral spaces are lined with sensitive mucosal tissue that provides us with information about the temperature and speed of the air passing by. This information, combined with kinesthetic information about movement in our torso, helps us to know how much air we have taken in and how much remains as we sing a phrase. In figure 14.1 we see that both spaces are quite deep, merging with the pharyngeal space just in front of the topmost vertebrae of the spine. The pharyngeal muscles are active during swallowing, constricting the pharyngeal space to move food downward. During breathing these muscles can rest as air passes through the pharyngeal space.

Sense

1. Using a hand mirror, examine your mouth. Explore the mobility of your lips, cheeks, tongue and soft palate. Notice the curved roof of your hard palate and the depth of the space from your front teeth to the back of your throat. Look at figure 14.1 and notice the proximity of your soft palate to your spine. Where are your jaw joints in relation to your palate?

2. Still watching in the mirror, say "ah" to raise your soft palate. Can you feel muscles lifting it from above? Figure 14.2 shows a cutaway of the vocal tract from behind. Palatal muscles on either side of the nasal passages lift the palate. Say [ŋ], the final sound in "sing," and your soft palate will drop as your tongue rises to meet it. Feel air flowing out your nose as you speak or sing this phoneme. What other sounds use nasal air flow?

3. Experiment with breathing slowly and quickly through your nose. Breathe through your mouth with various shapes, such as lips pursed and mouth wide open. Notice changes in the

temperature and speed of air passing across the sensitive mucosal tissue in your mouth and nose as you breathe.

4. Say a long [f] as in the word "fee," then inhale through that same [f] shape. Notice that the inhalation is noisy and that it requires more work to breathe through the resistance created by your top teeth and bottom lip nearly touching. Now say a long [ç] as in "hee" or "hue." Inhale through the [ç] shape, noticing the resistance to inhalation where your tongue and palate are so close together. Finally, say a long [h] as in the word "hay." Your vocal folds nearly close to create the friction for this sound. Inhale through the [h] space and notice the resistance and sound. Now allow the muscles of your vocal tract to rest as you breathe silently.

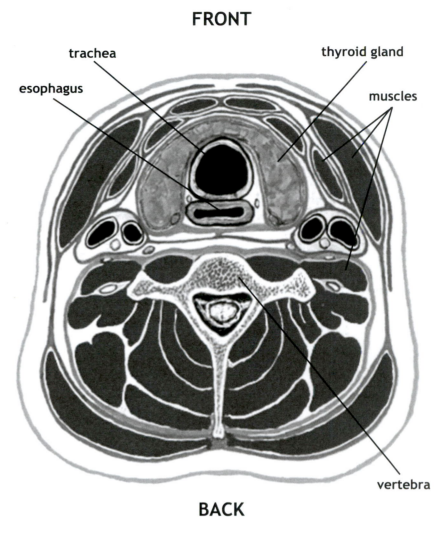

FRONT

trachea

esophagus

thyroid gland

muscles

vertebra

BACK

14.3 cross section of the neck

5. Figure 14.3 is a cross section of the neck just below the larynx. Use it as a guide as you explore your neck with your fingertips. Gently palpate your larynx and trachea just beneath the skin at the front of your neck. Feel the bumpy processes of your spinal vertebrae in back. Walk your fingertips all around the rest of your neck. Other than the larynx, trachea, and vertebrae, everything you feel is muscle. Notice whether these muscles are springy and relaxed. If they are tense, experiment with your skeletal balance to find greater ease here.

6. Take a drink of water, noticing movements of your tongue, soft palate and pharyngeal muscles as you swallow. Acknowledge that the water is passing through your esophagus, behind your trachea and larynx. After drinking, allow those muscles to relax completely as you breathe quietly. Repeat this exercise with food the next time you eat, attending to the movements of chewing and swallowing. After each bite, allow your muscles to relax as you breathe quietly. These muscles can rest when you breathe for singing, too.

XV. Expressive Ease - Your Arms

Expressive arms and hands convey emotion whether moving or resting comfortably at our sides. Even when they are still, lively arms participate in the whole-body patterns of micro-movement that are crucial to balance and breathing. When mistakes occur in our arm maps, the resulting tension interferes with ease and grace of movement. The arm structure is closely intertwined with the neck and upper torso, so arm tension affects those areas, too.

Figure 15.1, by the 18th century anatomist Albinus, shows beautifully poised and eloquent arms. How does this depiction of the bony structure of the arms differ from your arm maps? Do you imagine your own arms and hands to be so long and elegant? Do you include collarbones and shoulder blades in your arm maps?

Two important arm joints that are often mis-mapped are featured in figure 15.2. The upper arm bone and shoulder blade meet at the humero-scapular joint. This relatively shallow joint allows the upper

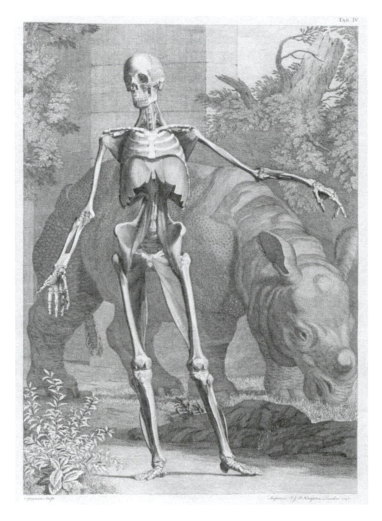

15.1 poised arms

arm to rotate and move in all directions. The sterno-clavicular joint, where the collarbone meets the sternum, is the only bony attachment of the arm to the torso. This joint allows the paired collarbone and shoulder blade to move all around, amplifying the range of motion of the whole arm.

The two long bones of the forearm appear in figure 15.3. When the arm is extended with the palm up, or supine, these bones are parallel. When the palm is facing down, or prone, the bones are crossed. Rotation of the hand takes place at the elbow, not at the wrist. Notice the eight bones of the wrist, which permit elegant bending and extension of the hand as well as side to side motion. The long bones of the hand, fingers and thumb allow great flexibility, dexterity and expressiveness.

What these images do not show is the vital support provided to the arms from above. Contrary to common belief, the shoulders do not sit on the ribs. Rather, the upper arm structure is

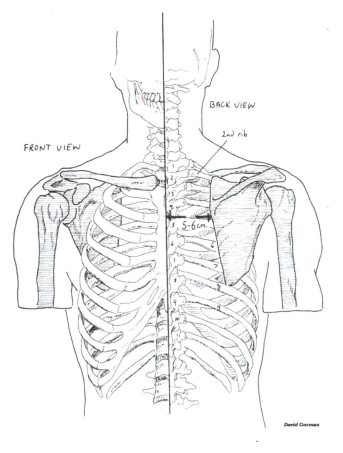

FRONT VIEW

BACK VIEW

2nd rib

5-6cm.

David Gorman

15.2 right arm (front and back view)

suspended from the skull and cervical spine by many layers of connective tissue. Strong and elastic, this translucent tissue is an important component of all muscles, providing tensile strength whether a muscle is contracted or released. Connective tissue in the neck and shoulder muscles support the collarbones and shoulder blades from above. Years of slouching or pulling the shoulders down and back will interfere with this support, but living tissue is resilient. Correcting body maps and moving with awareness go a long way towards regaining freedom in the arms. Additional resources are listed in the Appendix.

Balanced, buoyant arms glide easily above the moving ribs and other breathing structures. When the arm structure is beautifully balanced over the torso, the neck muscles are free to release and full range of motion is available to the ribs. Singers who claim the full length and mobility of their arms gain a world of expressiveness in vocal tone and physical presence.

Sense

1. With your right hand, feel your left collarbone. Walk your fingers along the collarbone to your sternum. Rest your fingertips on the end of your collarbone where it meets your sternum at the sterno-clavicular joint. As you gently move your left shoulder all around, notice the movement of your collarbone in the joint and all along its length. Palpate your sternum just below the collarbone to feel your first rib. Figure 15.2 illustrates the proximity of these two bones.

2. Now walk your fingertips to the far end of your collarbone, then onto your shoulder blade. Notice that your shoulder blade sweeps up and forward to meet your collarbone. The joint where these two bones meet is not mobile, so whenever your collarbone moves, so does your shoulder blade, and vice versa. Place your right hand atop your left shoulder so you can feel your collarbone and the top of your shoulder blade. Lift your left arm overhead and feel both bones raise simultaneously.

3. If possible, have a partner place his or her hands on your shoulder blades as you move, then trade places and repeat. Start with large swimming and flying motions. Feel your shoulder blades gliding over your ribs and your collarbones moving in their joints with the sternum. Now imagine a water spigot several feet in front of you at eye level. Gently reach forward with one hand, grasp and turn the imaginary handle, first clockwise, then counterclockwise. Notice that you can turn your hand a little bit without much movement of your upper arm. Turn it further, allowing the movement to be easy. The further you turn your hand, the more your upper arm, shoulder blade and collar bone will move, unless muscle tension prevents it. Repeat this hand-turning movement with your arms stretched out to the side, reaching overhead and down at your sides.

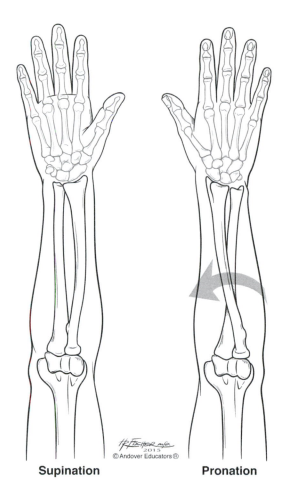

Supination   **Pronation**

15.3 right arm (supination and pronation)

4. Figure 15.3 shows the right forearm in supine and prone positions. Look at this image, then lay your right forearm and hand palm up on a flat surface. Without lifting your arm, flop your hand palm down then palm up a few times. You are moving between supination (palm up) and pronation (palm down). Notice that your pinky finger and the pinky side of your forearm can stay in contact with the table during this movement. The thumb side of your hand and forearm rotate over the pinky side as the long radius and ulna bones in your forearm cross and uncross. Use your kinesthetic and tactile senses to explore this rotation at the elbow.

Sing

Sing a favorite song while moving your arms. Include your shoulder blades and collarbones in large, sweeping movements that resemble swimming, flying and dancing. Bring awareness to all your arm joints as well as the large upper back and chest muscles that move your arms. Notice any changes in your breathing, vocal tone or mood. Gradually make your arm movements smaller, finally coming to stillness while allowing your arms, chest, back and neck to remain free and open.

XVI. Core Integration - Spinal Mobility

In this book we have explored the many singing structures nestled up along the full length of the spine, from the pelvic floor at the base to the soft palate at the very top of the spine. As the core organizing structure of the body, the spine plays a central role in breathing and in singing. To reach full potential, singers must have an accurate map of the spine that honors its innate mobility within the context of the whole moving body.

A balanced and supple spine will adjust in shape to enable easy movement of the ribs, diaphragm and organs. Spinal movement in breathing is often noticeable as a deepening of the thoracic curve; the thoracic spine moves back as the sternum rides forward and up with the ribs. Then, as the diaphragm releases upward and the ribs and sternum glide back down during exhalation, the spine will also rebound.

Figure 16.1 illustrates the unity of the diaphragm, ribs and spine in a view from below. If any part of this breathing trio moves, that movement will extend through the other structures of breathing and the whole body. The cyclical movement of breathing combined with the ongoing process of balancing keeps our skeleton in a state of continual micromovement, if we allow it. In addition to optimizing breathing, this natural mobility reduces strain on the nerves, discs and vertebrae and rejuvenates the whole body.

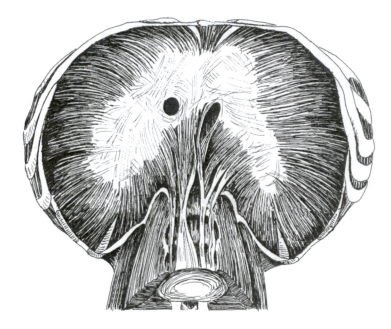

16.1 the diaphragm, ribs and spine from below

In Chapter 8 we learned about the webwork of connective tissue that unifies the body, integrating weight distribution and movement. When any part of the body moves, every other part responds, either fluidly or with resistance and rigidity. In a body free of restricting tension, spinal mobility is part of a whole-body pattern of movement accompanying the wave-like motion of breathing. This subtle yet powerful motion can be elusive for many singers. Some experience it as a sensation of internal buoyancy or elasticity. It is an involuntary movement that we permit and can encourage through dynamic balance and muscular freedom. Allow the natural springiness of your spine to enliven your breath!

Sense

During these explorations, at first you may feel spinal mobility only as subtle movement of your head or torso against the ball or pillow. If you don't feel it right away, don't be discouraged. As you release tension, spinal movement will increase spontaneously. The following exercises are reprinted by permission from Amy Likar's *The Breathing Book for Flute.*

Exploration on a ball:

You may want to have someone spot you on the ball when you try these for the first time. Kneel on the floor and drape over a physioball. Let your head turn to one side or the other—whatever is comfortable. Hug the ball gently. And breathe! Notice four phases of the breath cycle, inhalation, transition to exhalation, exhalation, and then the rest moment before the next inhalation enters. You can add some resistance to your exhalation by adding a slow hiss, but always being aware of keeping your jaw and neck free.

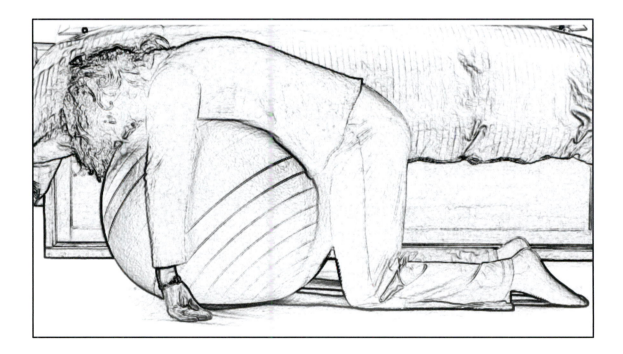

16.2 exploration on a ball

Explorations with a pillow:

Exploration One:

1. Lie face-down over a bed pillow. (I prefer using a king sized one.)

2. I also put some books with a washcloth over them under my forehead so that my head can feel supported and I don't have to turn my head to one side or the other.

3. Lie there and breathe and permit the four phases of the breath cycle as above and notice the mobility of your spine while you experience the movement of your ribs in the back. Because you are lying on your chest you may experience less movement in the front. You may also want to put pillows under your ankles for comfort.

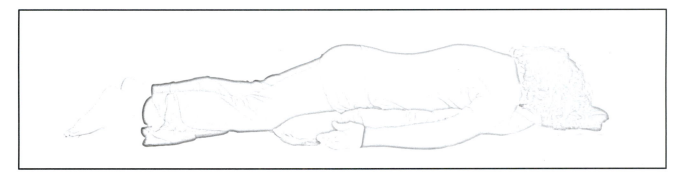

16.3 exploration one with a pillow

Exploration Two:

1. Lie on your side with the pillow between your knees. Again you can use a few books or your hand to support your head. Again permit your breath.

2. You will notice rib movement in the front, the back and the side that is up, and less movement on the side you are lying on. Repeat lying on the other side.

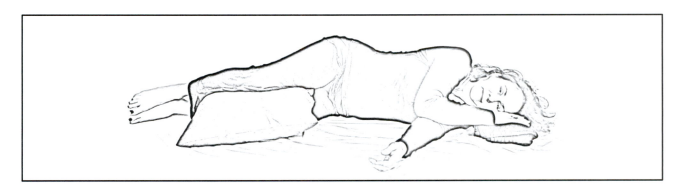

16.4 exploration two with a pillow

Exploration Three:

1. Lie on your back and place the pillow under your knees so that you do not have to hold your legs in any way.

2. Place a hand on your abdomen and chest; you may want more pillows to support your arms so that you don't have to hold them. Permit free and easy breath and notice the four cycles of breath, inhalation, transition to exhalation, exhalation and the rest before your next inhalation.

Sing

Exploration Four:

After all of that work on the floor, it's time to either sit or stand and explore this motion with your voice. As you sigh, hum or sing simple phrases, monitor the ease and quality of the movement of your ribs and see if you can sense ease and mobility in your spine as you sense the mobility of your ribs. The work you did draping over a ball or pillow makes it easier to sense the mobility of your spine and ribs. This movement is much more subtle when you are actually singing. The keys to observing spinal mobility are to be mindful of how your torso and legs are interacting, making sure your torso is up and over your pelvis and hip joints and cultivating awareness of what is happening deep inside your body as you sing. Be observant, be balanced and sing free of tension in your body, and you can learn to appreciate the enormous benefit of spinal mobility!

XVII. Putting It All Together

The human being is a miracle of dynamic, cohesive structure. When we move with clear intention, aware of our self and honoring the interconnectedness of our whole body, great things are possible. However, when we think of the body as a collection of pieces and parts that can be manipulated individually, problems occur. The fact is that a small change in one place may cause an imbalance or improvement elsewhere in the body.

For example, while we may not initially think of our legs as important to breathing, figure 17.1 clearly shows the relationship of the upper leg to the diaphragm. The psoas muscle flexes and rotates the femur at the hip joint and also acts on the lumbar spine. You can see that its attachments to the spine are adjacent to those of the diaphragm. Imbalance in the legs or feet can be communicated upward through the psoas, interfering with efficient movement of the diaphragm as well as overall skeletal balance. Finding balance and freedom in the legs, or almost any area of the body, has the potential to dramatically improve breathing.

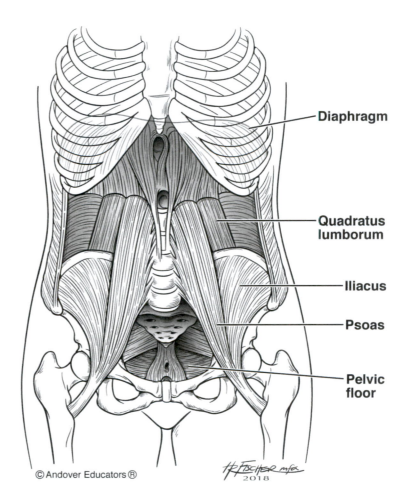

© Andover Educators ®

17.1 upper leg/diaphragm relationship

Labels: Diaphragm, Quadratus lumborum, Iliacus, Psoas, Pelvic floor

There are so many elements interacting in support of excellent breathing that it may seem overwhelming to think of them all. In fact, in the moment of activity it is not possible to direct the movement of each individual part. Trying to do so can even be destructive, particularly in performance situations. Instead, we can set ourselves up for success by ensuring that we have adequate, accurate body maps and clear movement intentions. Then we can allow spontaneous movement to realize our musical ideas. When we inhale for a phrase, inspiration prompts a cascade of coordinated movements, including contraction of the diaphragm, movement of the ribs and spine and abduction of the vocal folds. As we sing, the rebound of abdominal and pelvic muscles, gradual release of rib muscles and movements in the vocal tract all occur in service of our musical ideas. These movements and their musical results are included in our unified field of attention, allowing us to respond when necessary to return to our ideal movement and sound.

The organization of our awareness is as crucial to good movement as physical integration. When we experience rich, inclusive perception of our physical body, our surroundings, our thoughts and emotions, the possibilities seem limitless. We can sing with ease through our entire vocal range, embody a character convincingly or move an audience simply with our physical presence. In Chapters Four and Six we explored several avenues for developing such awareness. Another way is through daily practice of constructive rest, which is an effective tool for releasing tension, balancing the body and expanding awareness.

The guide to constructive rest that follows is condensed from a session led by Barbara Conable at the University of Colorado-Boulder in 2014. Consider having a partner read the instructions to you the first few times you practice. For a more complete experience read the full transcript. You will find a link in the Appendix, along with other resources.

FIVE TASKS OF CONSTRUCTIVE REST

Begin constructive rest in semi-supine position, on your back with your knees softly bent. Search for the leg position that feels balanced and easy. If you are too injured or tense to be in supine position, do constructive rest seated or draped over a therapeutic ball until you are comfortable lying down. You may want to support your head with a book or some other object to accommodate neck tension that will later be released.

Task one of constructive rest is the cultivation of an integrated body awareness. You might begin by bringing all your tactile, or touch, sensation into awareness. Continuing to build body awareness, find your kinesthetic sensation. As you let yourself be fully aware of your position, your moving, and your size, you will learn whether you are tense or relaxed, whether you are symmetrical or twisted. Kinesthetic and tactile experience ranges from miserable through delicious. If you're uncomfortably tense, just let yourself be aware of it. Awareness is the means to change.

Next, look to be sure that all your emotions are in awareness, in all their complexity and intensity. Now, add to all your tactile, kinesthetic, and emotional awareness anything other: pain, pleasure, hunger, thirst, anything. It is this bringing together of all experience in a single gestalt that we call integrated awareness: all the discrete bits of information are in relation to each other. Your attention can shift easily among the items in awareness. Some come into focus as others lie on the periphery of attention.

Task two is coming to the greatest degree of muscular freedom you can find in the moment. Using your body awareness, let yourself register any tensions in your body. You may find that you automatically begin to free out of tension as you become aware of it. If your neck is nicely free and not imposing tension on the rest of the body, then just enjoy the freedom and see if there are other tensions you may release. Awareness is key to release. Intention is the means.

Task three is to work on breathing, using your body awareness and increasing freedom. Typically, people continue to free muscularly as they enhance rib movement and abdominal wall and pelvic floor movement. It's a virtuous circle: releasing muscles restores breathing; breathing well frees muscles. Does breathing involve a long, easy sweep of movement top to bottom in the torso, on both inhalation and exhalation? If not, you may be manipulating your abdominal wall without even knowing that you are, interfering with coordination. Enjoy the excursion of your ribs up and out on inhalation and then follow the movement down and in on exhalation. Ask yourself whether you are allowing the full excursion down and in. Now explore the movement of your abdominal wall, front, sides and back. Are you allowing the full movement of the abdominal wall all around in breathing, or is there tension that is interfering? Now explore pelvic floor movement in breathing. You want to be certain there is no interference from tension there so that the pelvic floor can be pushed downward on inhalation, and so that the pelvic floor can spring back as the pressure from the viscera comes off. In singing, that rebound provides one aspect of breath support.

Task four is cultivating an accurate, adequate body map. As before, secure your body awareness, find muscular freedom, breathe beautifully, and then work on the integrity of your body map. If your body map is already accurate and adequate to your purposes, you may want to refine it, make it more detailed. If not, simply move on to task five.

Task five. Work on your relationship to space and time. Look all around and put yourself in relationship to everything you see. Let your hearing help you by registering every sound. Use your tactile sense to tell you about the space, for instance, the nature of the floor. Let your emotions live in relationship to the space. Notice that you can claim for your moving any amount of space you choose. Many people learn as they claim larger spaces for their movement that much of their former tension came from the small, bubble-like space they were confined to earlier. Constructive rest is the perfect opportunity to train oneself to perceive time - for musicians this is the stuff of rhythm - and claim it as one's own.

When you finish any session of constructive rest, make no effort to keep its benefits. That would just introduce some strain. Just get up and go about your business, knowing that your brain will assimilate the experience of constructive rest. That's its job.

XVIII. Moving Ahead

Now that you have explored this entire book, you may have made some major neurological changes. Ideally, you have begun refining your skeletal and respiratory maps and developed more accurate kinesthetic awareness as part of a larger field of inclusive attention. Through these changes, you may have already found greater ease in your sitting, standing, breathing and singing.

Because each facet of your being interacts with all the rest, attending to one area of your body often brings new awareness or changes to other areas. If you are uncomfortable at times or find that you revert to concentration in moments of stress, do not worry. These problems are normal parts of the somatic process. It takes time to change your brain. Keep practicing to make inclusive attention and physical balance part of your daily life. Continue to correct and refine your body maps. Celebrate improvements in your breathing and your sound as you practice and perform.

The goal of Body Mapping is easy movement in support of our intentions. As noted earlier, the process of Body Mapping may be quick for some people. A lucky few might already have adequate and accurate body maps. For most of us, though, Body Mapping can be a lifelong process of examining, correcting and refining our body maps and cultivating inclusive attention. These tools allow us to harness the power of neuroplasticity to improve our movement even as we learn new skills, recover from injury and continue along life's path.

As you become more discerning in your movement sense, you may notice imbalances of which you were previously unaware. At any time, you may return to pertinent pages or look in the Appendix for resources to help you continue to refine your body maps. It can also be helpful to return periodically to the places of balance introduced in Chapter Five. Below are several of my favorite exercises, focusing on the central, base and topmost points of balance. Return to these etudes daily, weekly or monthly as you continue to refine your body maps. As you explore balance and buoyancy with these exercises, remain aware of your quality of attention. Allow your focus to shift as needed while you remain aware of your whole body, your thoughts, feelings and voice, and the space, sights and sounds around you.

We all created our maps in infancy and childhood through exploration. Returning to that state of child-like curiosity about movement and sensation allows us to repair and refine our maps. Can you approach this work as though it is play? Allow your whole self to be engaged. Enjoy!

~ *Balance at the Center*

1. Sit comfortably balanced on the edge or corner of a chair or piano bench. Feel your skull balanced over your spine and your long, strong spine balanced over your pelvis. Feel the contact of your sitting bones with the surface of your seat. Now slowly rock back on your sitting bones. Allow your spine and skull to move along with your pelvis, as though your sitting bones were the rockers of a rocking chair and your spine were the back of the chair. Hold this rocked-back position for a moment and notice the work that your abdominal muscles are doing to hold you up. If you released them now you would fall backwards. Slowly rock forward to upright, allowing your abdominal muscles to release completely as you come to balance. Let go of any work you feel in your neck, back and legs as you explore balance.

2. After a moment, rock forward on your sitting bones, again allowing your spine and skull to come along as depicted in figure 18.1. Notice work in the muscles of your back, legs and buttocks as they keep you from tipping forward off your seat. Now rock slowly back to upright, releasing your muscles in back as you come to balance. Allow the weight of your head and torso to be delivered by your spine to your pelvis and by your pelvis to the chair. Allow your legs to be free.

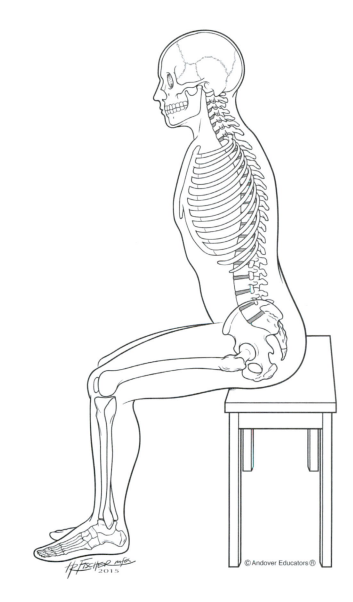

18.1 leaning forward in balance upright

3. Remind yourself that balance is not a position to be held, but a state through which you move continually. As you enjoy seated balance, notice how the movement of breathing subtly affects your balance at the level of your pelvis, skull and arms.

4. Repeat this exercise and allow your attention to expand. How does moving away from and returning to balance over your seat affect your skull balance, the freedom of your tongue or jaw muscles, your arms, feet, breath and emotions?

~ *Balance at the Base*

1. Stand and find a comfortable balance of your whole skeleton over your feet, noticing how your weight is distributed over the heels and balls of your feet as well as from side to side. Bring your focus to each of the main places of balance: knees, pelvis, feet, lumbar spine, arms and skull. As you bring your whole body into balance, allow those muscles under your conscious control to release as your bones bear your weight and deliver it to the floor.

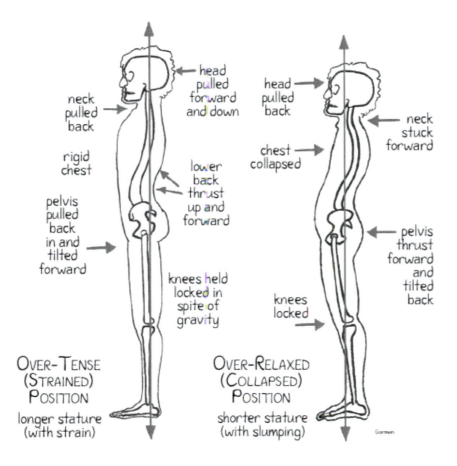

neck pulled back

rigid chest

pelvis pulled back in and tilted forward

head pulled forward and down

lower back thrust up and forward

knees held locked in spite of gravity

OVER-TENSE (STRAINED) POSITION
longer stature (with strain)

head pulled back

neck stuck forward

chest collapsed

pelvis thrust forward and tilted back

knees locked

OVER-RELAXED (COLLAPSED) POSITION
shorter stature (with slumping)

Gorman

18.2 strained and collapsed postures

2. Try out the "collapsed" posture in figure 18.2. Feel the contact of your feet with the floor. Is your weight centered? Notice how standing this way feels in your body and how it affects your breathing.

3. Move your body into the "strained" posture in figure 18.2. Notice how this position affects your breathing and legs and the contact of your feet with the floor.

4. Bring yourself to balance. Allow your weight to be distributed evenly through your feet. How does this balanced state feel in your body? How does it influence your breathing?

~ *Balance at the Top*

1. Sitting comfortably balanced, allow an expansive awareness that includes your self and your surroundings. Bring your focus to the relationship of your skull and spine. Allow your neck and jaw muscles to soften as the weight of your skull transfers easily through your spine, downward through your pelvis and is delivered to your seat. If your abdominal, back or leg muscles are active, look for balance over the pelvis that will allow them to release.

2. From balance, tip your head back slightly to look up. Notice how this movement affects your whole body. Which muscles engage? If you released muscles in the front of your neck, would your head fall back? Are leg and abdominal muscles holding your torso upright? After a few moments, bring your head back up to balance. Allow your muscles to release as your bones deliver your weight downward to the chair.

3. Now tip your head forward slightly, looking down. Notice muscles in the back of your body working to keep your torso from tipping forward. Once again, return to upright and balance as you allow your muscles to release.

4. Remind yourself that balance is the state from which movement in any direction is easiest. When you release habitual muscular tension, automatic postural reflexes call upon small muscles nestled around your core to continually bring you back into balance. As you breathe, your balance is shifting continually. Tune in to your kinesthetic sense to become aware of small movements in your joints as you breathe, as you sit, as you stand and as you sing.

Appendix

If you wish to delve more deeply into anatomy, sensory awareness or other elements of somatic study, there are many resources available. This list presents some of my favorites.

Books and Apps:

What Every Musician Needs to Know About the Body
Barbara Conable presents essential information about the body in music-making with numerous illustrations, concise explanations, and witty, memorable sayings. Excellent for musicians who don't want to read a lot of text.

What Every Singer Needs to Know About the Body
Now in its third edition, this book by veteran Andover Educators Melissa Malde, Kurt-Alexander Zeller and MaryJean Allen presents detailed explorations of various aspects of the singing voice through the lens of Body Mapping. Extensive information about physical structures, alignment, breathing, phonation, resonance, gesture and articulation with numerous illustrations and experiential exercises.

How to Learn the Alexander Technique
Barbara Conable's practical guide to the Alexander Technique incorporates principles of Body Mapping and contains information specific to actors, dancers and musicians.

The Anatomy of Breathing
Blandine Calais-Germaine's excellent illustrations and clear explanations are accessible and concise, making this book invaluable for anyone who wants a deeper understanding of breathing. Experiential exercises in the back of the book explore various types of breathing and offer pathways for optimizing breathing through movement and awareness. Other books by Calais-Germaine are equally compelling and immediately applicable to movement.

The Body Moveable
David Gorman presents the human body in detailed illustrations and intelligent, thorough prose. Detailed attention to function alongside structure sets this book apart.

The Anatomy Coloring Book
Wynn Kapit's book enables the reader to begin immediately integrating anatomical knowledge into one's own self-representation through coloring.

Essential Skeleton
This free, stand alone app does not contain any in-app purchase requirements and delivers outstanding 3D views of skeletal anatomy.

Biotensegrity: The Structural Basis of Life
Graham Scarr provides a detailed view of the body through the lens of biotensegrity, an exciting new element of biomechanical theory.

Anatomy Trains
Tom Myers explores whole body integration through fascia in an accessible, well-illustrated text.

Discovering the Body's Wisdom
Although Mirka Knaster's comprehensive guide to more than 50 types of body work was published 22 years ago, it remains relevant when searching for a modality to meet your needs, such as myofascial release, the Feldenkrais method, Ayurveda, various styles of massage or martial arts.

Sensory Tune-Ups
Kay Hooper offers an experiential journal for personal exploration and development of the senses that musicians need to be fully expressive.

Video Clips and DVDs:

Move Well, Avoid Injury DVD
This video guide to mapping the body by Barbara Conable and Amy Likar contains immediately applicable exercises, explorations and images. The website www.movewellavoidinjury.com contains sample clips that serve as practical introductions to the process of Body Mapping.

The Art of Breathing DVD
Alexander Technique teacher Jessica Wolf provides elegant, clear and accurate 3D animations of the muscles, bones and organs of respiration.

"3D View of the Diaphragm" on YouTube - animation of the diaphragm and thoracic skeleton in breathing.

"3D Diaphragm Demo" on YouTube - animation showing interaction of the diaphragm, thoracic skeleton and organs from various angles.

"Science-Respiratory System" on YouTube - an animated tour of respiration all the way down to the cellular level.

"Tensegrity Torso" on YouTube - In this brief video, Tom Flemons' tensegrity model illustrates the interaction of rigid and tensile structures in motion.

"What Is Tensegrity" on YouTube - Tom Myers explains the physical foundations of integrated movement.

"Biotensegrity" on YouTube - dynamic model of the spine illustrates principles of biotensegrity and integrated movement.

Web Resources:

www.bodymap.org
The online home of Andover Educators, an international organization of music educators committed to saving, securing, and enhancing musical careers by providing accurate information about the body in movement. The site provides an in-depth look at Body Mapping through a wide variety of articles, including its scientific basis and early development; suggested reading; a complete directory of licensed teachers; calendar of courses and workshops.

www.musiciansway.com/wellness/
Gerald Klickstein offers an extensive list of resources for musicians seeking wellness, as well as a blog featuring articles such as "The 12 habits of healthy musicians."

www.claudiafriedlander.org
This blog contains articles about singing presented from a sound physiological perspective. Of particular interest are "The Pressures of Breathing" (*Classical Singer,* January 2016) and "Breathing Between the Lines."

www.tmj.org/Page/34/17
The "Living with TMD" page of The TMJ Association contains information about the jaw joints, TMJ Disorder, self care, and when and where to seek treatment.

http://muppet.wikia.com/wiki/Beverly_Sills?file=Beverlysills.jpg
Imagine Beverly Sills' quality of attention as you view this image of her performance on The Muppet Show.

www.colorado.edu/music/sites/default/files/attached-files/fivetasksofconstructiverestfinal.pdf
The full transcript of Barbara Conable guiding students in constructive rest during the Alexander Technique Summer Course at CU-Boulder, July 2014.

Index